Art of Team Building

Art of Team Building

A.K. Banerjee

Lotus PRESS

4735/22, Prakash Deep Building
Ansari Road, Darya Ganj,
New Delhi - 110002

Lotus Press : Publishers & Distributors
Unit No. 220, 2nd Floor, 4735/22, Prakash Deep Building,
Ansari Road, Darya Ganj, New Delhi- 110002
Ph.: 41325510, 9811838000
• E-mail : lotuspress1984@gmail.com
www.lotuspress.co.in

Art of Team Building

ISBN: 978-81-8382-210-7

Printed & Published by : **Lotus Press Publishers & Distributors,** New Delhi-02

PREFACE

The term team building generally refers to the selection, development, and collective motivation of result-oriented teams. More specifically, in the corporate scenario, the term team-building has implications which prove to be crucial to the efficiency and success of an organisation, since any corporate outfit is incomplete in its success without a coordinated team charcterised by unity. Teams are indispensable to the smooth functioning of an organisation, and as such, team-building is a process which holds the key to a better managed and more profitable organisation.

The present text has been designed as a manual which looks into the strategies and craft which goes into the construction of successful teams at the organisational level. The idea behind the book is to equip the new age manager with the skills and wherewithal to make an organisational team which can handle the stress and the pressure which comes with the corporate work, while simultaneously foster and maintain relationships within the team which can make work both enjoyable and profitable. Incorporated into the book are case studies which provide greater information on the subject, which should help the reader gain greater practical insight into the team-building.

It is hoped that the incisive content of the text serves well for all. Any suggestions for further improvement are most welocme.

Editor

CONTENTS

1

NATURE AND SCOPE OF TEAMS AND GROUPS

A team is a group of individuals working together to achieve a common goal. In most cases, the task is split into parts appropriate to each individual's talents. Each member of the team has a shared responsibility for getting the job done, and therefore their cooperation is essential to the overall success of the group.

WORK IN A TEAM

There are many reasons for working in teams within an organisation. Team effort produces better results when tackling unfamiliar problems by combining the knowledge and skills of each individual. The team provides an environment in which each individual has the opportunity to maximise their input to the task. Some of the advantages of teamwork are:

— *Typically informal atmosphere:* If the group meets on a regular basis, the members should start to feel at ease with each other and hence feel free to state their opinions openly.

— *Rapid commmunication:* With all the members of the team being in the same organisation, there is no delay in exchanging information and opinions between them. This makes it by far the most productive means of fulfilling the desired objective.

- *Fast decision-making:* This results from rapid communication and good leadership management. A group can frequently make the right decision quickly.
- *Instantaneous feedback:* As a group meeting is a real-time face-to-face situation, opinions, thoughts and decisions from each member can be given straight away.
- *Wide range of skills:* The larger the group, the more extensive the variety of knowledge and skills which can be pooled together.
- *Increases responsibility:* Each individual's responsibilities can be increased. They can be given the responsibility for getting a specific task completed.
- *Higher quality results:* Groups have the advantage of receiving mutual feedback between members; each individual's contribution is analysed by the other members of the team. By using the resources available and constantly improving the way in which the tasks are approached, higher quality and increased productivity can be achieved.
- *Synergy:* The drive and motivation realised within a group as a whole is greater than the sum of each individual's within the group.

GROUP

When a number of people are gathered in one place, interacting with one another, and working as a team, different people will assume different roles. Three general roles have been identified:

- *Doers:* People performing this role may be initiating ideas or taking leadership of the group. They will concentrate on the actions required and be willing to make decisions.

- *Thinkers*: Perhaps less dominant members of the group, thinkers will digest all the information and ideas before coming to a conclusion. They fulfil an evaluation role and take time to reflect upon different ideas.
- *Carers:* These people want to ensure that the task is performed correctly and will consider logistical issues associated with the implementation of any ideas. They may also assume the role of "finisher" and speed up the decision-making process so that the task is completed on time.

The fulfilment of all the different roles in the group can be considered to be necessary if the task is to be completed in the most successful manner.

Problems within Groups

Bringing together a number of people with different personalities, skills, experiences and opinions to form a team can affect their ability to achieve a common goal. Problems can arise from the social interaction between members or through poor team management. Some of the main factors affecting the group performance are:

Domination

Strong personalities can seriously affect the group's initial line of thinking and stifle innovative ideas from less dominant members. A group having a number of dominant personalities may transform their meetings into monologues between themselves—defeating the purpose of forming the group.

Quiet members

Those who do not feel involved in the discussion or those

with a quiet personality may actually come up with the best suggestions and be the most experienced in a particular area.

Distractions

Caused by an unusual setting, a windowed meeting-room or side conversations. Can affect the communication between members and the flow of the decision-making process?

Over-management

If the team leader controls the meeting too tightly, only a couple of opinions will be discussed; and group members will not feel free to make innovative suggestions. Individuals could suffer from a lack of motivation linked to not being responsible for decisions relating to their tasks.

Personality clashes

This is a major and difficult problem to solve. In some cases this may result in suggestions constantly being ridiculed or arguments developing about insignificant or irrelevant points. Communication and cooperation between team members will suffer and affect group morale and performance.

Unclear roles and responsibilities

If some roles within the team are unfilled or team members are not sure of what they are responsible for, some tasks will not be completed and the work coordination of the team will suffer.

Communication problems

If a team member has difficulties explaining what he/she means, this can result in misinterpreted points or suggestions. If he/she misunderstands their delegated task, this can be the worst case, result in the final task not meeting the specification. In any case, valuable time will be wasted towards the completion of the task.

Lack of clarity

During meetings and delegation of tasks, objectives that are not sufficiently explained and decisions that are not clear and concise may result in the completed task not meeting the specification. The team members may feel less motivated because they do not know exactly what is happening within the group.

Time management

It is important that the time available for a meeting is used as effectively as possible. Time costs money, and it is thus vital that meetings do not overrun. Therefore, it is vital that some control is placed on the time allocated to each part of the meeting—the team leader must accept this responsibility.

Lack of background knowledge

There is no point in delegating a task to a team member if he/she does not possess the knowledge or ability to carry out the task.

Groups that Work

Groups form a basic unit of work activity throughout engineering and yet the underlying process is poorly managed. When people work in groups, there are two quite separate issues involved. The first is the task and the problems involved in getting the job done. Frequently, this is the only issue which the group considers. The second is the process of the group work itself: the mechanisms by which the group acts as a unit and not as a loose rabble. However, without due attention to this process the value of the group can be diminished or even destroyed; yet with a little explicit management of the process, it can enhance the worth of the group to be many times the sum of the worth of its individuals. It is this synergy which makes group work attractive in corporate organisation despite the possible problems (and time spent) in group formation.

A group of people working in the same room, or even on a common project, does not necessarily invoke the group process. If the group is managed in a totally autocratic manner, there may be little opportunity for interaction relating to the work; if there is factioning within the group, the process may never evolve. On the other hand, the group process may be utilised by normally distant individuals working on different projects.

In simple terms, the group process leads to a spirit of cooperation, coordination and commonly understood procedures and mores. If this is present within a group of people, then their performance will be enhanced by their mutual support. If you think this is a nebulous concept when applied to the world of industry, consider the opposite effect that a self-opinionated, cantankerous loud-mouth would have on your performance and then contrast that to working with a friendly, open, helpful associate.

Importance of Groups

Groups are particularly good at combining talents and providing innovative solutions to possible unfamiliar problems; in cases where there is no well established approach/procedure, the wider skill and knowledge set of the group has a distinct advantage over that of the individual.

In general, however, there is an overriding advantage in a group-based workforce which makes it attractive to Management: that it engenders a fuller utilisation of the workforce. A group can be seen as a self-managing unit. The range of skills provided by its members and the self-monitoring which each group performs makes it a reasonably safe recipient for delegated responsibility. Even if a problem could be decided by a single person, there are two main benefits in involving the people who will carry out the decision. Firstly, the motivational aspect of participating in the decision will clearly enhance its implementation. Secondly, there may well be factors which the implementer understands better than the single person who could supposedly have decided alone.

More indirectly, if the lowest echelons of the workforce each become trained, through participation in group decision-making, in an understanding of the companies objectives and work practices, then each will be better able to solve work-related problems in general. Further, they will also individually become a safe recipient for delegated authority.

From the individual's point of view, there is the added incentive that through belonging to a group each can participate in achievements well beyond his/her own individual potential. Less idealistically, the group provides an environment where the individual's self-perceived level of responsibility and authority is enhanced, in an environment where accountability is shared: thus providing a perfect motivator through enhanced self-esteem coupled with low stress. Finally, a word about the much vaunted "recognition of the worth of the individual" which is often given as the reason for delegating responsibility to groups of subordinates.

Group Development

It is common to view the development of a group as having four stages:

- Forming.
- Storming.
- Norming.
- Performing.

Forming is the stage when the group first comes together. Everybody is very polite and very dull. Conflict is seldom voiced directly, mainly personal and definitely destructive. Since the grouping is new, the individuals will be guarded in their own opinions and generally reserved. This is particularly so in terms of the more nervous and/or subordinate members who may never recover. The group tends to defer to a large extent to those who emerge as leaders.

Storming is the next stage, when all Hell breaks loose and the leaders are lynched. Factions form, personalities clash, no-one concedes a single point without first fighting tooth and nail. Most importantly, very little communication occurs since no one is listening and some are still unwilling to talk openly. True, this battle ground may seem a little extreme for the groups to which you belong - but if you look beneath the veil of civility at the seething sarcasm, invective and innuendo, perhaps the picture come more into focus.

Then comes the *Norming*. At this stage the sub-groups begin to recognise the merits of working together and the in-fighting subsides. Since a new spirit of co-operation is evident, every member begins to feel secure in expressing their own view points and these are discussed openly with the whole group. The most significant improvement is that people start to listen to each other. Work methods become established and recognised by the group as a whole.

Performing is the culmination, when the group has settled on a system which allows free and frank exchange of views and a high degree of support by the group for each other and its own decisions.

In terms of performance, the group starts at a level slightly below the sum of the individuals' levels and then drops abruptly to its nadir until it climbs during Norming to a new level of Performing which is (hopefully) well above the start. It is this elevated level of performance which is the main justification for using the group process rather than a simple group of staff.

Group Skills

The group process is a series of changes which occur as a group of individuals form into a cohesive and effective operating unit. If the process is understood, it can be accelerated. There are two main sets of skills which a group must acquire:

- Managerial Skills.
- Interpersonal Skills.

As a self-managing unit, a group has to undertake most of the functions of a Group Leader - collectively. For instance, meetings must be organised, budgets decided, strategic planning undertaken, goals set, performance monitored, reviews scheduled, etc. It is increasingly recognised that it is a fallacy to expect an individual to suddenly assume managerial responsibility without assistance; in the group it is even more so. Even if there are practiced managers in the group, they must first agree on a method, and then convince and train the remainder of the group.

As a collection of people, a group needs to re-learn some basic manners and people-management skills. Again, think of that self-opinionated, cantankerous loud-mouth; he/she should learn good manners, and the group must learn to enforce these manners without destructive confrontation.

Accelerating Development

It is common practice in accelerating group development to appoint, and if necessary train, a "group facilitator". The role of this person is to continually draw the groups' attention to the group process and to suggest structures and practices to support and enhance the group skills. This must be only a short-term training strategy, however, since the existence of a single facilitator may prevent the group from assuming collective responsibility for the group process. The aim of any group should be that facilitation is performed by every member equally and constantly. If this responsibility is recognised and undertaken from the beginning by all, then the Storming phase may be avoided and the group development passed straight into Norming.

The following is a set of suggestions which may help in group formation. They are offered as suggestions, no more; a group will work towards its own practices and norms.

Focus

The two basic foci should be the group and the task. If something is to be decided, it is the group that decides it. If there is a problem, the group solves it. If a member is performing badly, it is the group who asks for change. If individual conflicts arise, review them in terms of the task. If there is initially a lack of structure and purpose in the deliberations, impose both in terms of the task. If there are disputes between alternative courses of action, negotiate in terms of the task.

Clarification

In any project management, the clarity of the

specification is of paramount importance - in group work it is exponentially so. Suppose that there is a 0.8 chance of an individual understanding the task correctly (which is very high). If there are 8 members in the group then the chance of the group all working towards that same task is 0.17. And the same reasoning hold for every decision and action taken throughout the life of the group.

It is the first responsibility of the group to clarify its own task, and to record this understanding so that it can be constantly seen. This mission statement may be revised or replaced, but it should always act as a focus for the groups deliberations and actions.

The Mouse

In any group, there is always the quiet one in the corner who doesn't say much. That individual is the most under utilised resource in the whole group, and so represents the best return for minimal effort by the group as a whole. It is the responsibility of that individual to speak out and to contribute. It is the responsibility of the group to encourage and develop that person, to include him/her in the discussion and actions, and to provide positive reinforcement each time that happens.

The Loud-mouth

In any group, there is always a dominant member whose opinions form a disproportionate share of the discussion. It is the responsibility of each individual to consider whether they are that person. It is the responsibility of the group to ask whether the loud-mouth might like to summarise briefly, and then ask for other views.

The Written Record

Often a decision which is not recorded will become clouded and have to be re-discussed. This can be avoided simply by recording on a large display each decision as it is made. This has the further advantage that each decision must be expressed in a clear and concise form which ensures that it is clarified.

Feedback (negative)

All criticism must be neutral: focused on the task and not the personality. So rather than calling Romy an innumerate moron, point out the error and offer him a calculator. It is wise to adopt the policy of giving feedback frequently, especially for small things—this can be couched as mutual coaching, and it reduces the destructive impact of criticism when things go badly wrong. Every criticism must be accompanied by a positive suggestion for improvement.

Feedback (positive)

If anyone does something well, praise it. Not only does this re-enforce commendable actions, but it also mollifies the negative feedback which may come later. Progress in the task should be emphasised.

Handling Failure

The long-term success of a group depends upon how it deals with failure. It is a very British tendency to brush off failure and to get on with the next stage with no more than a mention—it is a very foolish tendency. Any failure should be explored by the group. This is not to attribute blame, but rather to examine the causes and to devise a mechanism which either monitors against or prevents repetition. A mistake should only happen once if it is treated correctly.

One practise which is particularly useful is to delegate the agreed solution to the individual or sub-group who made the original error. This allows the group to demonstrate its continuing trust and the penitent to make amends.

Handling Deadlock

If two opposing points of view are held in the group then some action must be taken. Several possibly strategies exist. Each sub-group could debate from the other sub-group's view-point in order to better understand it. Common ground could be emphasised, and the differences viewed for a possible middle or alternative strategy. Each could be debated in the light of the original task. But firstly the group should decide how much time the debate actually merits and then guillotine it after that time - then, if the issue is not critical, toss a coin.

Sign Posting

As each small point is discussed, the larger picture can be obscured. Thus it is useful frequently to remind the group: this is where we came from, this is where we got to, this is where we should be going.

Avoid Single Solutions

First ideas are not always best. For any given problem, the group should generate alternatives, evaluate these in terms of the task, pick one and implement it. But most importantly, they must also monitor the outcome, schedule a review and be prepared to change the plan.

Active Communication

Communication is the responsibility of both the speaker and the listener. The speaker must actively seek to express the ideas in a clear and concise manner—the listener must actively seek to understand what has been said and to ask for clarification if unsure. Finally, both parties must be sure that the ideas have been correctly communicated perhaps by the listener summarising what was said in a different way.

Group Facilitation

To facilitate is:

- To free from difficulties or obstacles.
- To make easy or easier.

or

- To carry out a set of functions or activities before, during and after a meeting to help the group achieve its own objectives.

Advantages of Group Facilitation

- Productivity.
- Group motivation, commitment and confidence.
- Better climate for radical change.
- Optimised group dynamics.

Role of Facilitator

To sum-up, the role of facilitator is as follows:

The facilitator is there to ensure a productive group process whether this is brainstorming a new idea or discussing the latest employee appraisals. The facilitator has a role within the group which comes down to the three following headings. The role of the facilitator is to ensure that the group works as a constructive and cohesive unit. This task has three parts:

Leadership

- *Focus:* To provide a focus for the group when the leader fails to fulfil their role.
- *Stimulate:* To encourage constructive debate between group members.

- *Support:* To bring out information from introverted members of the group and to allow new ideas to be submitted.
- *Participate:* When the group is interacting poorly or in the wrong direction the facilitator must be willing to promote new discussion.
- *Team building:* To form a cohesive, interactive and productive team.

Referee

- *Regulation:* To maintain order of the group discussion, discouraging participants from talking at the same time, or dominating the floor.
- *Protect members:* To ensure that all contributions to the discussion are treated equally and that no-one is rebuffed for their input.
- *Deal with problems:* To control problem people within the group allowing everyone to participate freely.
- *Timekeeper:* To adhere to the meeting timetable thus ensuring completion of the agenda.

Neutral

- *Pragmatic:* To take a detached look at the discussion viewing each point on its merits.
- *Encourage feedback:* To promote discussion of each point raised, by all members of the group.
- *The facilitator:* must be a neutral to the discussion, taking a pragmatic view of all points raised. This frees the facilitator to concentrate on the group rather then the content of the discussion and hence they can ask pertinent and stimulating questions.

Managerial Skills and Qualities

To be effective in the role of a facilitator the person needs to be effective as a manager, requiring several skills and qualities to be able to guide the meeting smoothly.

- *Communication:* The ability to put over points using all the techniques available both verbal and non verbal, receptive listening is also an important tool.
- *Planning:* To arrange the venue for the meeting and to set it up in such a way that all barriers are removed between facilitator and audience. The time allocation to the meeting has to include time for discussions and feedback sessions.
- *Leadership:* To forge a team from a group of individuals through motivation and empowerment of the individuals. Delegation of tasks is essential to being a good leader also knowing when to stand back and let the team have its head and when to take the initiative.
- *Training:* Based upon knowing what the team needs to ensure that it becomes an efficient and effective unit. This is achieved through evaluation of the strengths and weaknesses of the individual members.
- *Problem identification:* Knowing that there is a problem is not enough you have to be able to get to its root cause be it human or mechanical. Both can be assessed via brainstorming and analysis sessions with the team or on an individual basis.
- *Consulting:* The facilitator cannot just stand up and give a formal lecture to the audience. They need to involve the audience and let them know what is going to be on the agenda. To get the audience to participate they need to be a catalyst for discussion and where necessary reform points made and feed it back to the audience to think about.

2

IMPORTANCE OF TEAMWORK

The concept of teamwork is extremely important to the success of any team. All coaches talk about working as one unit, as a unified team. Teamwork and unselfishness create the backbone of a great team, without them a team cannot realistically compete. You can have a group of superstars, but if they do not work well as one unit, chances are they are not going to be as successful as you would think. The team working as one cohesive unit is going to be the key in their success. Here are some things to take into consideration when you are looking at your team:

1. Does your team have agreed-upon goals they created as a team?
2. Do the players openly encourage and support one another?
3. Do they have open communication with one another, as well as the coaching staff?
4. Does each player know what their role on the team is?
5. Is there mutual respect among the players and coaching staff?

6. Do players use statements such as "we" when referring to the team, or is it more of an "every man for himself" mentality?
7. Have they created a positive team image for themselves?
8. Are the individual contributions of each player recognised?
9. Is the team as a whole committed to improving performance?
10. Does each member consider themselves as a "team player?"

A productive team has players that share common goals, a common vision and have some level of interdependence that requires both verbal and physical interaction. Teams come into existence through shared attitudes about a particular sport. They may come together for a number of different reasons, but their goals are the same—to achieve peak performance and experience success. The ends may differ but the means by which one gets there is the same—teamwork. Every member of the team is accountable when it comes to teamwork.

To succeed at the task in hand everyone involved needs to combine their efforts. If everyone does their job well, then it increases what the team can accomplish. This teamwork has to be recognised by everyone and know that great things can happen if individuals master the fundamentals and work together as one unit. Everyone has their own unique role, but each person's individual role must be recognised and appreciated.

Teamwork is something that must be a high priority and given constant attention. Every player needs to understand how important it is for them to work smoothly together if they want to be successful. Each player must be dedicated to the whole team and be willing to act unselfishly. When challenges arise, the team needs to have the resources, accountability and commitment to deal with them in a constructive and positive manner. A sense of teamwork will play an integral part in this.

Teamwork "a joint action by three people or more or a group of people, in which each person subordinates his or her individual interests and opinions to the unity and efficiency of the group."

This does not mean that the individual is no longer important; however, it does mean that effective and efficient teamwork goes beyond individual accomplishments. The most effective teamwork is produced when all the individuals involved harmonise their contributions and work towards a common goal.

In order for teamwork to succeed one must be a teamplayer. A teamplayer is one who subordinates personal aspirations and works in a coordinated effort with other members of a group, or team, in striving for a common goal. Businesses and other organisations often go to the effort of coordinating team building events in an attempt to get people to work as a team rather than as individuals.

The forming-storming-norming-performing model takes the team through four stages of team development and maps quite well on to many project management life cycle models, such as:

— initiation,

— definition,

— planning, and

— realisation.

As teams grow larger, the skills and methods that people require grow as more ideas are expressed freely.

Managers must use these to create or maintain a spirit of teamwork change. The intimacy of a small group is lost, and the opportunity for misinformation and disruptive rumours grows.

Teamwork is essential for competing in today's global arena, where individual perfection is not as desirable as a high level of collective performance. In knowledge based enterprises, teams are the norm rather than the exception. A critical feature of these team is that they have a significant degree of empowerment, or decision-making authority. There are many different kinds of teams: top management teams, focused task forces, self-directed teams, concurrent engineering teams, product/service development and/or launch teams, quality improvement teams, and so on.

Not all groups in organisations are teams, but all teams are groups. The difference between a team and a group is that a team is interdependent for overall performance. A group qualifies as a team only if its members focus on helping one another to accomplish organisational objectives. In today's quickly changing business environment, teams have emerged as a requirement for business success. Therefore you should constantly try to help groups become teams and facilitate the evolution of groups into teams.

The purpose of assembling a team is to accomplish bigger goals than any that would be possible for the individual working alone. The aim and purpose of a team is to perform, get results and achieve victory in the workplace and marketplace. The very best managers are those who can gather together a group of individuals and mould them into a team. Here are ten key differentials to help you mould your people into a pro-active and productive team.

1. *Understandings:* In a group, members think they are grouped together for administrative purposes only. Individuals sometimes cross purpose with others. In a team, members recognise their independence and understand both personal and team goals are best accomplished with mutual support. Time is not wasted struggling over "Turf" or attempting personal gain at the expense of others.
2. *Ownership:* In a group, members tend to focus on themselves because they are not sufficiently involved in planning the unit's objectives. They approach their job simply as a hired hand. "Castle Building" is common. In a team, members feel a sense of ownership for their jobs and unit, because they are committed to values-based common goals that they helped establish.
3. *Creativity and contribution*: In a group, members are told what to do rather than being asked what the best approach would be. Suggestion and creativity are not encouraged. In a team, members contribute to the organisation's success by applying their unique talents, knowledge and creativity to team objectives.
4. *Trust:* In a group, members distrust the motives of colleagues because they do not understand the role of other members. Expressions of opinion or disagreement are considered divisive or non-supportive. In a team, members work in a climate of trust and are encouraged to openly express ideas, opinions, disagreements and feelings. Questions are welcomed.
5. *Common understandings:* In a group, members are so cautious about what they say, that real understanding is not possible. Game playing may occur and communication traps be set to catch the

unwary. In a team, members practice open and honest communication. They make an effort to understand each other's point of view.

6. *Personal development:* In a group, members receive good training but are limited in applying it to the job by the manager or other group members. In a team, members are encouraged to continually develop skills and apply what they learn on the job. They perceive they have the support of the team.
7. *Conflict resolution:* In a group, members find themselves in conflict situations they do not know how to resolve. Their supervisor/leader may put off intervention until serious damage is done, i.e. a crisis situation. In a team, members realise conflict is a normal aspect of human interaction but they view such situations as an opportunity for new ideas and creativity. They work to resolve conflict quickly and constructively.
8. *Participative decision-making:* In a group, members may or may not participate in decisions affecting the team. Conformity often appears more important than positive results. Win/lose situations are common. In a team, members participate in decisions affecting the team but understand their leader must make a final ruling whenever the team cannot decide, or an emergency exists. Positive win/win results are the goal at all times.
9. *Clear leadership:* In a group, members tend to work in an unstructured environment with undetermined standards of performance. Leaders do not walk the talk and tend to lead from behind a desk. In a team, members work in a structured environment, they know what boundaries exist and who has final authority. The leader sets agreed

high standards of performance and he/she is respected via active, willing participation.

10. *Commitment:* In a group, members are uncommitted towards excellence and personal pride. Performance levels tend to be mediocre. Staff turnover is high because talented individuals quickly recognise that:
    (*a*) Personal expectations are not being fulfilled,
    (*b*) They are not learning and growing from others, and
    (*c*) They are not working with the best people.

In a team, only those committed to excellence are hired. Prospective team members are queuing at the door to be recruited on the basis of their high levels of hard and soft skill sets. Everyone works together in a harmonious environment.

Whether in the workplace or on the football field, or even amongst members of a community, effective teamwork can produce incredible results. However, working successfully as a team is not as easy as it may seem. Effective teamwork certainly does not just happen automatically; it takes a great deal of hard work and compromise. There are a number of factors that must be in place to cohere together as a team and work seamlessly.

- *Good leadership:* Effective leadership is one of the most important components of good teamwork. The team's leader should possess the skills to create and maintain a positive working environment and motivate and inspire the team members to take a positive approach to work and be highly committed. An effective team leader will promote a high level of morale and make them feel supported and valued.

- *Clear communication:* Communication is a vital factor of all interpersonal interaction and especially that of a team. Team members must be able to articulate their feelings, express plans and goals, share ideas and see each other's viewpoints.
- *Establishing roles:* It is absolutely necessary for team members to understand what their role on the team is, what he/she is responsible for. The team leader can enable this by defining the purpose in a clear-cut manner in the beginning of the formation of the team.
- *Conflict resolution:* Conflicts will arise no matter how well a team functions together. The best way to counter conflict is to have structured methods of conflict resolution. Team members should be able to voice their concerns without fear of offending others. Instead of avoiding conflict issues, a hands-on approach that resolves them quickly is much better. It is often advised that the team leader sit with the conflicting parties and help work out their differences without taking sides and trying to remain objective if possible.
- *Set a good example:* The team leader must set a good example for good teamwork to come about. In order to keep team members positive and committed and motivated, the team leader herself/himself needs to exhibit these qualities. The team looks to the leader for support and guidance so any negativity on the leader's part can be disastrous.

Regardless of what type of sales you are in, you may one day be asked to be part of a team sales effort, and knowing how to effectively work on and with a team is going to be crucial to your success and that of your team.

Teamwork in the company has great importance for more than one reason. Companies, who have embraced the concept, have reported increased performance in work production, problem solving and has stimulated new growth. This group project approach has improved employee morale and increased input when managed correctly. The benefits of teamwork can make a positive effect in the company that incorporates this type of teamwork approach. Resources must be available within the company or outsourced by businesses who will come in and train their employees to make the most effective effort.

One format of teamwork utilised by the company is the Self-Directed Team. Within this group a leader is assigned by management or elected by the group. The team leader must be effective early on if the group project is to be completed on schedule. He/she must be intuitive as to each team member's strength and weaknesses of knowledge and skills when assigning work needed to begin and progress to complete projects. Group projects can be short term or long term. An example of a short-term project would be devising a new marketing presentation for the debut of a new product being added to the list of products made by the company. A long term project would be continuous testing of products sold by the company to develop cost saving improvements.

As each new project is started, a new team leader may be assigned. The reason for this is with each new project the area of expertise needed may change. These teamwork groups are helpful to the manager. By delegating the responsibility of a project to the designated group, it lessen his/her workload with confidence the group project will be done correctly and on time with only minute participation needed from him/her. The high performance of these teams make the use of group teamwork an important part of the company's work ethics.

Attributes an employee needs to have to be a productive member on a team are the ability to be a team player and possess the knowledge and skills necessary to complete their assigned portion of the work task. After completion of their portion, the employee should be willing to assist other team members with completion of all work tasks until the project is completed. Without these major attributes the team will flounder and be less productive. This is the main reason teamwork is so very important to the success of the company, because a company is only as qualified and deserving as the employees it hires and trains.

CREATE A CULTURE OF TEAMWORK

Want to make your next team building activity or team building exercise live up to its true potential? Integrate the team building with real-time work goals. Establish a systematic workplace integration and follow-up process—before you go on the team building adventure. You need to make the good feelings and the outcomes from the team building activity last beyond the final team building exercise.

Without this attention to integration, corporate team building or planning events are, at best, a short term boost to employee enthusiasm and positive morale. If they are planned and executed well, people feel good about themselves and about each other. Employees get to know each other better and have a common experience to talk about back at work.

A frequent expectation from team building activities is that they build trust. Team building events have little to do with building trust, however, unless company planning, that is carefully followed up on and yields real results, is part of the team building or retreat.

At worst, team building sessions help employees become cynical about their organisations. This occurs when the team building events are held outside of the context of the company's normal way of doing business. If you send people off to a team building event, as an example, but all rewards in your company are based on individual goals and efforts, the team building event will have no lasting impact.

People will lose productive hours complaining about the time and energy invested in the team building or planning activities. Unhappiness, management criticism and employees complaining to each other sap energy, productivity and joy from the work day.

An event that is not followed up with meaningful activities in the workplace should not be held. They harm trust, motivation, employee morale and productivity. They don't solve the problems for which they were scheduled and held. You will eventually lose the people you most want to keep—especially if they don't see your organisation getting better as a result of off-site team building and planning sessions.

If the team building event has no follow up, people become jaded about such events as a waste of time and energy. The success of a team building or of a strategic planning activity begins well before the start of the sessions. Use a team to plan the event since you want to model the behaviour you seek from the team building sessions you schedule. The likely long-term effectiveness of a team building event or corporate retreat is enhanced when you incorporate annual team building events into an overall company structure. This cultural framework of philosophies, values and practices is designed to build the concept of "team" on a regular basis. In this environment, team building sessions can yield supportive results.

If team building and other offsite events are to offer value, their inclusion in an overall corporate structure of philosophies, values and practices is critical. People must already operate in a team-oriented environment that is characterised by such philosophies as shared purpose, shared vision, shared mission and a performance development system that enables people to grow both personally and professionally. Or, your organisation must be proactively pursuing team work as a business and employee strategy.

In such a system, team behaviours are rewarded and recognised. Teams solve problems and improve processes. There is a genuine concern for employees and the policies and work are employee and employee-family friendly. When a problem or failure occurs, the search is not for the guilty, but instead, managers ask, "What about the work system caused that person or team to fail?"

When such a structure exists on an ongoing basis within an organisation, team building events can enhance and help the system grow stronger. Again, build the team building events around a business purpose to which all attendees can contribute, and you have the opportunity for an energising, exciting growth opportunity.

Successful companies regularly demonstrate their commitment to building team unity, trust and positive morale among their employees in their daily workplace. Without this commitment and the presence of team building success factors, negative effects can result from formal team building or planning sessions.

Team building and planning events and activities have the potential to bring the people you employ a strong sense of direction, workable plans and solutions, a powerful feeling of belonging with and on the team and clear, strategic customer-focused values.

Poorly planned and executed, created outside of the context of the total organisation, the team building and planning sessions bring disillusionment, low morale and negative motivation. They fail to deliver the results expected. Organisations flounder with little strategic direction. Everyone works hard, but, usually on the wrong tasks and goals. Employees take baby steps toward accomplishing key action items and nothing important is finished.

Fostering teamwork is creating a work culture that values collaboration. In a teamwork environment, people understand and believe that thinking, planning, decisions and actions are better when done cooperatively. People recognise, and even assimilate, the belief that "none of us is as good as all of us."

It's hard to find work places that exemplify teamwork. In America, our institutions such as schools, our family structures, and our pastimes emphasize winning, being the best, and coming out on top. Workers are rarely raised in environments that emphasize true teamwork and collaboration.

Organisations are working on valuing diverse people, ideas, backgrounds, and experiences. We have miles to go before valuing teams and teamwork will be the norm.

You can, however, create a teamwork culture by doing just a few things right. Admittedly, they're the hard things, but with commitment and appreciation for the value, you can create an overall sense of teamwork in your organisation.

To make teamwork happen, these powerful actions must occur.

- Executive leaders communicate the clear expectation that teamwork and collaboration are expected. No one completely owns a work area or process all by himself. People who own work processes and positions are open and receptive to ideas and input from others on the team.

- Executives model teamwork in their interaction with each other and the rest of the organisation. They maintain teamwork even when things are going wrong and the temptation is to slip back into former team unfriendly behaviour.
- The organisation members talk about and identify the value of a teamwork culture. If values are formally written and shared, teamwork is one of the key five or six.
- Teamwork is rewarded and recognised. The lone ranger, even if she is an excellent producer, is valued less than the person who achieves results with others in teamwork. Compensation, bonuses, and rewards depend on collaborative practices as much as individual contribution and achievement.
- Important stories and folklore that people discuss within the company emphasize teamwork. People who "do well" and are promoted within the company are team players.
- The performance management system places emphasis and value on teamwork. Often 360 degree feedback is integrated within the system.

TIPS FOR TEAM BUILDING

Do you immediately picture your group off at a resort playing games or hanging from ropes when you think of team building? Traditionally, many organisations approached team building this way. Then, they wondered why that wonderful sense of teamwork, experienced at the retreat or seminar, failed to impact long-term beliefs and actions back at work.

You will not build teamwork by "retreating" as a group for a couple of days each year. Think of team building as something you do every single day.

– Form teams to solve real work issues and to improve real work processes. Provide training in systematic methods so the team expends its energy on the project, not on figuring out how to work together as a team to approach it.

– Hold department meetings to review projects and progress, to obtain broad input, and to coordinate shared work processes. If team members are not getting along, examine the work processes they mutually own. The problem is not usually the personalities of the team members. It's the fact that the team members often haven't agreed on how they will deliver a product or a service or the steps required to get something done.

– Build fun and shared occasions into the organisation's agenda. Hold pot luck lunches; take the team to a sporting event. Sponsor dinners at a local restaurant. Go hiking or to an amusement park. Hold a monthly company meeting. Sponsor sports teams and encourage cheering team fans.

– Use ice breakers and teamwork exercises at meetings. Participants took turns bringing a "fun" ice breaker to the meeting. These activities were limited to ten minutes, but they helped participants laugh together and get to know each other—a small investment in a big time sense of team.

– Celebrate team successes publicly. Buy everyone the same t-shirt or cap. Put team member names in a drawing for company merchandise and gift certificates. You are limited in teamwork only by your imagination.

Take care of the hard issues above and do the types of teamwork activities listed here. You'll be amazed at the progress you will make in creating a teamwork culture, a culture that enables individuals to contribute more than they ever thought possible—together.

Team is "two or more people who must coordinate their activities to accomplish a common goal". The common goal and the required coordination make them a team. It is not enough for people to want to coordinate because it would be nice. Coordination must be required to accomplish the task in order to be a team.

BENEFITS OF TEAMWORK

The main value of teams is their ability to assemble and empower employees to use their talents to improve the organisation. In more fully participating in decisions and planning how work will be performed, employee contribution and, for most, job satisfaction are increased. Why teamwork?, because it improves:

- Quality.
- Flexibility.
- Coordination.
- Satisfaction and Development.
- Productivity/Cost.

Essentials of a Team

- A "Charter" Mission—reason for working together.
- Interdependency.
- Commitment to benefits of group problem solving/ decision making.
- Accountability as a Functioning Unit.

CREATING POWER TEAMS

1. Defining the mission. A mission is your team's ultimate purpose.
   - Why do we exist?
   - Who do we serve?
2. Communicating the Vision and Formulating Overarching Goals.
   - A vision is something to aspire to. It is not a mystical thing, but a practical thing. The vision is, a way of communicating the organisation's strategy and objectives so that they excite people, challenge people and attract them.
3. Developing a Code of Ethics.
   - How are we going to behave toward one another?
   - Which are the team's values?
4. Establishing Roles.
   - Functions.
   - Authority.
   - Accountability.
   - Priorities.
5. Blending Individual Styles.
   - Utilising strengths, minimising weaknesses.
   - Motivating various styles.
   - Managing conflict successfully.
6. Managing team performance conflict successfully.
   - Determining success criteria.
   - Formulating a Consensus and "By-In."
   - Performing a Resource Audit.

7. Evaluating the success criteria.
8. Marketing the team.
9. Celebrating success-recognition.
10. Action-Planning.

FACTORS IN TEAM DEVELOPMENT

In the end, we describe some factors in team development. They are:

- *Commitment:* Team members see themselves as belonging to a team rather than as individuals who operate autonomously. They are committed to group goals above and behind their personal goals.
- *Trust:* Team members have faith in each other to honour their commitments, maintain confidences, support each other, and generally behave in a consistent and predictably acceptable fashion.
- *Purpose:* The team understands how it fits into the overall business of the organisation. Team members know their roles, feel a sense of ownership, and can see how they make a difference.
- *Communication:* Communication refers to the style and extent of interactions both among members and between members and those outside the team. It also refers to the way that members handle conflict, decision making, and day-to-day interactions.
- *Involvement:* Everyone has a role in the team. Despite differences, team members must feel a sense of partnership with each other. Contributions are respected and solicited, and a real consensus is established before committing the team to action.
- *Process orientation:* Once a team has a clear purpose, it must have a process or means to get there. The

> process should include problem-solving tools, planning techniques, regular meeting, meeting agendas and minutes, and accepted ways of dealing with problems.

Despite our cultures emphasis on individuals, teamwork still pays a big part in our corporate environment. Only those who work for themselves, and by themselves, in cottage industries are truly on their own. All of the rest of us have to cope with other people to get things done. Customers rely on businesses to produce goods and services. In turn, bosses rely on their employees, and employees have to rely on their team-mates to get projects done by the time they are due. If we all said, "The heck with teamwork," the entire economy would grind to a halt.

The key to teamwork is putting the needs of the project over one's own petty desires and cares. It is the goal that matters, not the individual. It is harder than it looks. If you don't, you will be fired long before you hit a position of power. After you make it to the top, you may not look like a good team player, at least from the views of the trenches, but that is just because your project goals are no longer the same as theirs.

There is a vast amount of difference between making a widget every hour, and how to make the most cost effective widget. The team making widgets on the assembly line are only concerned with putting the product together. The team supervising the assemblers are concerned with market placement, the competition, pricing and how to make the most profit. As one moves up though the ranks of a company, the team that you are on changes, and so does the goals that you are concerned with.

To be the most effective team member, learn what your team's goal is. Periodically, review it to see if it is still current. If you move to another team, learn what their goal is.

Also remember a large part of teamwork is getting along with other people. If a group of people is pulling in different directions, then less is going to be accomplished.

The importance of teamwork is that it allows us to accomplish more than we could by ourselves. It allows us to move mountains. If you doubt the importance of teamwork, just ask yourself where Bill Gates would be today without his team and the work they did.

3

BASICS OF TEAM BUILDING

An organisation is composed of a group of individuals that have come together out of mutual interest. Each person brings to the group his or her special talents, history, skills, unique set of experiences and a set of norms or values. Team building shifts the focus of the group to its members rather than the organisational tasks, thus allowing the members to feel important and cared for.

It is the group process that uses activities requiring members to work together to discover shared interests and lays the groundwork for new and deeper friendships. When done effectively, team building highlights each person's differences in values, personality and skills while simultaneously building the membership into a cohesive, trusting and mutually supportive group. Building strong interpersonal ties increases member satisfaction and group productivity. Team building should not be used in an attempt to make everyone the same.

There are many different methods of team building, each designed to produce differing results. If this is the first time your organisation paying close attention to the expected results. If this is first time your organisation will be participating in a team-building process, you might find it better to pick one of the less risky exercises. You can always choose a riskier exercise after you have been working together for a while and are more comfortable as a group.

Whatever you select, it is important to emphasize both the group and individual benefits gained through team-building. Never force a member to participate. Not all people are comfortable participating in an activity that requires self-disclosure; they will when they feel it is time.

After you have completed your team building exercise, it is necessary to spend time as a group discussing this experience. Part of any team building process is sharing what has been learned and experienced; what members liked and disliked; and, most importantly, how they felt while participating. Team-building is hindered if inadequate time is allotted for discussion or if individual feelings surface and are not dealt with.

Although team building is essential to newly formed groups or an organisation with a large number of new members, there are other times it can be effective as well. You might find it helpful to use team building techniques when

- Members seem bored or irritable.
- Members appear to be going off in different directions or drifting away from the group.
- There is a great deal of conflict or infighting.
- Members have been apart for a while (vacations, breaks, etc.)
- You want to take a break from the normal routine or boost team spirit.

EXAMPLES OF TEAM BUILDING EXERCISES

Self-disclosure/relationship building helps break down

the barriers and allows members to get to know one another on a more intimate level. It is very appropriate for groups where people will be working together closely and/or for groups where members will be together for long periods of time.

Intimate interviews: Members pair off and interview one another for five minutes each. One of the partners introduces the other to the group speaking in the first person as if he or she were the person being introduced.

Personal crest: Members make a personal coat-of-arms in which they express important aspects about themselves through drawings or short phrases. Possible topics or questions to include in the crest: the most significant event in your life; how you react when upset; your primary goal for the year; where you would like to be in five years.

Trust exercises: Generally rely on some form of physical contact but have the added element of requiring participants to trust one another in order to complete the activity. They are appropriate in most any group; but be careful that if someone is really afraid, he/she is not pressured into participating.

Trust walks: Members take turns being blindfolded and led by another on a short walk.

Trust falls: Members stand on a raised platform or chair and fall backwards into the arms of the other members.

Physical exercises: Help eliminate tension and distance between people, and make them more relaxed and comfortable with each other. These are appropriate in most groups; but beware of individual reactions to touching/being touched.

Human knot: Members stand in a circle and extend their right hands into the middle and clasp the hand of another. Repeat using the left hand. Untangle the knot without unclasping hands.

Cooperation exercises: Help people learn to work together. These exercises can give an indication about the roles members will play in group situations. These are appropriate in any group particularly if tasks demand teamwork.

Perfect square: Squares of construction paper of different colours are cut into odd shapes. Members each take a piece and then work with others who have the same colour to form a perfect square. This exercise is often done in silence without talking permitted.

Brainstorm: Members are asked to contribute ideas regarding a specific problem or question facing the group. Ideas are recorded without judgement. Group Goal-Setting: members participate in reviewing and setting the group's goals and objectives. People are more committed to a course of action they helped to choose.

Other: Parties, potlucks, meals and retreats help break the monotony of regular meetings and provide an opportunity for members to get back in touch with each other on a social basis. These are appropriate anytime in a group and are particularly helpful when motivation is lacking, morale is low, or members are drifting apart.

GOAL SETTING

Goals are statements describing exactly what your organisation wishes to accomplish. They are the ends towards which your efforts will be directed. However, it is very important to review these goals periodically; and it is very normal to change them from term to term or even year to year. The timing will depend on your particular organisation. When reviewing your goals, you should keep in mind the following:

- Do they fit with the overall purpose of the group?
- What is the status of membership currently?
- How does the group stand financially?
- What new programmes can realistically be accomplished?

Bear in mind that your goals should be realistic, attainable and measurable.

Objectives are descriptions of exactly what is to be done in order to meet and reach your goals. They are concise, clear statements of exactly what you plan to accomplish. They are short-term, measurable, and attainable over a specified period of time. It is quite normal to have several or even quite a few objectives for each goal.

Many leaders wonder why goals are so important. The reason is clear: they help define your organisation; they give direction; and they help assist your organisation in avoiding mild chaos. They can help motivate members by clarifying and communicating what the organisation is striving to achieve. They are also great for membership recruitment by allowing potential members to know what your group is all about. They could also be considered time savers by helping members and leaders become aware of problems in time to develop solutions. They help organisations plan ahead and be prepared. But best of all, they are a basis for recognising accomplishments and realising your successes. The following represents some steps for setting goals and developing an action plan:

- It is best to set goals as a group. This will create many positive results because people support what they help to create. You can expect from your members:

  - Better commitment.
  - More motivation among members and officers.
  - Better understanding of the goals and the rationale for selecting them.
  - Better goals as a result of having more ideas and opinions in the decision process.
- Brainstorm goals as a group.
- Prioritise your goals as a group.
- Determine objectives for each goal and plan of action for each objective.
- Move into action.
- Evaluate your progress on a regular basis.
  - Remember that circumstances change, so be flexible and allow your objectives to change with them.
  - A good way to review what you accomplish is by placing your goals on a large sheet of poster board and marking through them as they are accomplished. This visually shows your group that you are on the way towards success.

Once your organisation has written its goals and objectives, it is now time to take the task one step further and develop an action plan. This could be defined as the actual mapping out in detail of what should be accomplished in a specific time frame.

- What is to be accomplished (your objective)?
- How will it be accomplished?
- What are your resources in terms of people, money, and materials?
- Who is responsible for completing each task?
- When will it be accomplished?

- How will you know when it has been accomplished?
- How will you measure it?

Example of an Action Plan

- **Goal**
  - To improve membership recruitment, retention, and involvement.
- **Objective**
  - To develop a committee structure whose purpose is to increase member involvement by at least 70% by next term.
- **How**
  - Brainstorm ideas to increase member involvement. Review your list and weed out either impractical or impossible ideas.
  - Discuss this edited list with the executive board of leadership. Determine which will be done and delegate the final process of setting up the final system to one or two officers.
- **Resources**
  - Members.
  - Executive officers.
  - Handouts on motivation, recruitment, delegation.
  - Your organisation's advisor.
- **Who**
  - Executive board.
  - Consultants.
- **When**
  - By next term.

  - Try to set a specific date if possible.
- **Results**
  - Acceptable–membership involvement increases by 40-70%.
  - Unacceptable–membership involvement increases by less than 40%.
  - Better than expected–membership involvement increases by more than 70%.

BRAINSTORMING

Brainstorming can and will get everyone excited and involved in your club or organisation. The purpose is to get out as many ideas as possible—the more you have to choose from, the better your final choice will be!! You can use brainstorming for almost anything—themes, programme ideas, problem-solving, publicity, slogans and group goals. The rules for brainstorming are obviously simple; be sure the group understands them and someone has the job of making sure they are followed.

First of all, you must set the stage:

- Set a time limit of 10-20 minutes, depending upon the complexity of the issue and the size of the group.
- The best group size is 3-15 people. If you have more, break into two or more groups and brainstorm simultaneously.
- The question or issue must be one to which all participants can speak. It is important to focus on only one issue.
- Record all responses on a chalkboard or big sheets of newsprint so everyone can see them; don't record the name of the person suggesting. Record only key words and phrases.

Second of all, explain the following "rules":

- Do not discuss ideas.
- Do not criticise, praise or judge.
- Be spontaneous—no hand raising, just call out.
- Repetitions are OK.
- Quantity counts.
- Build on each other's ideas.
- Enjoy the silences—often the best ideas come out of them - It's okay to be outrageous, even silly.

Third of all, make good use of your members' creativity:

- If several groups brainstormed the same idea, put the lists on the wall and let everyone read each other's work.
- Group ideas into related categories for review.
- Decide which ideas are most promising and which can be eliminated.
- Rank order the most promising.
- Select those with the greatest potential and high-ranking priority for either implementation or refinement by committee.
- Be sure to utilise the ideas generated. It is extremely demoralising for a group to invest its time, energy and creativity and its ideas disappear. On the other hand, seeing your idea come to fruition is extremely rewarding.

BREAK THE ICE

The primary goal for an icebreaker or getting acquainted exercise is the development of an environment which is anxiety reducing and allows individuals the opportunity to get acquainted with each other by having fun.

Icebreaker exercises should be used with any group that appears to be extremely anxious in the initial stage of development, i.e., first meeting of clubs, programme boards, etc.

Icebreakers should not be used to avoid dealing with anxiety but rather to provide your members with a less threatening environment. A non-threatening environment initiated at the beginning of development may make way for more meaningful interaction during the life of the group. Bear in mind the following about icebreakers and getting acquainted exercises:

- They can be excellent devices to help members feel more comfortable with themselves and with others and feel more "at home" in a group.
- They break up the "cliques," invite people to form random groupings, and help individuals meet others in a non-threatening and fun way.
- They can be used to set a tone for the time a group will be together, to encourage people to feel "safe" and hopefully to evoke lots of laughter in releasing tension.

Getting acquainted exercises could include:

- *Dyads:* Members get into groups of two and find out information about each other. Possible questions to use:
  - Who do you think is the most important person who has lived in the past 100 years?
  - What is the best movie you have seen recently?
  - What is the title of the last book you read?
  - If you could be any animal other than human, what would you be?
  - If you could travel to any place in the world, where would you go?

- What is your favourite sport?
- One adjective to describe me is....
- The emotion I find most difficult to control is....

- *Crest or coat of arms:* Members create their own coat of arms by filling in information about themselves using words or drawings. Information can include:
  - Hobbies.
  - Hometown.
  - Major.
  - Favourite Emotion.
  - Family Members.
  - Five or Ten Year Goals.
- *Forced choice:* Ask members to stand in the middle of the room and have them move to either side to indicate their choice.
  - More like a Santro or a Ford Ikon?
  - More like a saver or a spender?
  - More like Mumbai or Bangalore?
  - More yes or no?
  - More like a student or a teacher?
  - More here or there?
  - More religious or non-religious?
  - More like the present or the future?
  - More like a file cabinet or a liquor chest?
  - More intuitive or rational?
  - More like a tortoise or a hare?
  - More like a roller skate or a pogo stick?
  - More like a bubbling brook or a placid lake?

CONFLICT MANAGEMENT

Conflict is inevitable in any interpersonal relationship or among members of any group. While we encounter various types of conflict in many of our life situations, we often feel a lack of confidence and vision of what is really appropriate to do. Most students find the conflict in their personal relationships already quite stressful; thus any conflict within student organisations becomes overwhelmingly unbearable. Those who have a lower tolerance level for anxiety often choose to leave the organisation.

Why do we shy away from dealing with our conflict? It is often because many of us were raised to believe that conflict is something to be avoided, an experience of failure. However, conflict does not have to lead to failure or even to the termination of a relationship. We all come to see and experience the world in a different way, and we all have different ideas about what is best for "my group" or "our group." Recognising this fact can help free us from the negative conclusion that conflict is a signal of failure. It is actually a signal that change is needed and even possible.

Ability to manage conflict is probably one of the most important social skills an individual can possess. This handout is designed especially to assist you in developing this skill. Specifically, it has three purposes:

- To help you raise your consciousness of the different ways in which people deal with conflict.
- To help you increase the awareness of your own style of conflict management.
- To discuss a constructive method of conflict management which not only will lead to greater satisfaction of both parties involved, but also will promote growth and development of your group.

These are several styles of conflict management that people use, some of which are more effective than others.

Competing: An individual pursues his or her own concerns at the other person's expense. This is a power-oriented mode, in which one uses whatever power seems appropriate to win one's own position: one's ability to argue, one's rank, or economic sanctions. Competing might even mean standing up for your rights, defending a position which you believe to be correct, or simply trying to win.

Accommodating: The opposite of competing. When accommodating, an individual neglects his or her own concerns to satisfy the concerns of the other person; there is an element of self-sacrifice in this mode. Accommodating might take the form of selfless generosity or charity, obeying another person's order when one would prefer not to, or yielding to another person's point of view.

Avoiding: The individual does not immediately pursue his or her own concerns or those of the other person. He or she does not address the conflict. Avoiding might take the form of diplomatically sidestepping an issue, postponing an issue until a better time, or simply withdrawing from a threatening situation.

Compromising: The objective is to find some expedient, mutually acceptable solution which partially satisfies both parties. It falls on a middle ground between competing and accommodating. Compromising gives up more than competing but less than accommodating. Likewise, it addresses an issue more directly than avoiding, but does not explore in as much depth as collaborating. Compromising might mean splitting the difference, exchanging concessions, or seeking a quick middle-ground position.

Collaborating: The opposite of avoiding. Collaborating involves an attempt to work with the other person to find some solution which fully satisfies the concerns of both persons. It means digging into an issue to identify the underlying concerns of the two individuals and to find an alternative which meets both sets of concerns. This is clearly the most effective approach of conflict management. Specifically it will produce the following results:

— Both sides win.

— Satisfaction.

— Mutual respect.

— Both parties feel enriched rather than belittled.

— Continuing effort of both parties.

Collaborating Approach in Student Organisations

Diagnosis is definitely the starting point—determining the nature of the conflict.

— *Is the issue a value conflict?* It is extremely difficult to negotiate when the conflict is in the philosophical arena. An example: a dispute about whether alcohol should be prohibited in a fund raising dance.

— *Is the issue a difference of expectations?* The extent of understanding this type of conflict lies in the fact that each of us has different expectations which grow out of our experiences with the organisation. Therefore, when we interact with others whose expectations have grown out of their own unique experiences with the organisation, conflicts arise.

Initiation is the second step.

— The most effective way to confront another in a conflict situation is to state the tangible effect a conflict has on you. Example: "We have a concern in our committee. Due to your stand on keeping a low budget for the officer transition retreat, we are unable to have the retreat off campus, which is the desire of most members."

Active listening is the third step. Negotiators must be capable of hearing the other person's point of view.

- While listening, do not think about how to reply in order to persuade.
- Argument provoking replies should be avoided.
- Active listening involves paraphrasing or restating what the other says. Ideas or content should be considered as well as feelings.

Problem-solving is the final step.

- Clarify the problem. After the above steps, each party should have a clear idea about what is the tangible issue.
- Talk about what is needed or wanted (be clear on facts and information).
- Generate a list of possible solutions. While doing this, let go of the solutions that you thought you had. This is the opportunity to be creative!!! The best negotiator makes the other side feel good. Start by thinking "How can I make the other side happy?"
- Decide together on the best solution acceptable to all parties. Do not try to persuade or coerce.
- Plan the implementation of the solution, make assignments of the who, what, where, when and how involved.
- Plan an evaluation or review of the solution after a specified period of time.

All five styles of conflict management obviously have advantages and disadvantages. When dealing with conflict in personal relationships, any of these types may be useful and necessary in certain situations. However, the last style, collaboration, is highly recommended for dealing with conflict in student organisations. It has the most promise of resulting in something satisfactory to both parties. People often feel proud of themselves and feel a sense of personal power when they use this method. It is a sign of integrity and self-confidence when one is able to use this method with patience, regardless of how difficult the situation may be.

Two issues which you may have to deal with when confronting a conflict:

People who will not negotiate: Some people refuse to negotiate because they want to protect their special interests and privileges. Here are a few steps to use when dealing with those people:

— Start to negotiate anyway.

— Explain why it is in their best interest to negotiate and why it is worthwhile for them to deal with the existing problems between you.

— Talk about problems that are theirs and how the collaboration will help solve them.

— Make it their problem. For example, bring to their attention the joint image that your subgroups project for the organisation.

When trust is an issue: Here are a few suggestions for this problem:

— Be trustworthy. Do what you said you would do.

— Find a higher value you both agree on. For example, you both want to project your group image.

- Listen.
- Make an agreement in such a way that you know when it is carried out.
- Start small.
- There are people who simply can't/won't trust you, but do your best anyway.

GROUP DECISION-MAKING

Combining your Energies

Student organisation members and leaders make decisions in the group all the time. The decision-making process could be stressful because some members see it as a form of power struggle; some people cannot bear the idea of losing an argument; and some people simply do not like to make decisions.

Decisions are an important part of group life, and you may wonder how your group could improve in this area. There are several types of group decisions such as

- *Unilateral:* A decision made by one person, often the nominal leader without consultation with other group members. At times it can be inappropriate; these decisions usually carry a very low group commitment.
- *Handclasp*: Decisions made by two members. One suggests, the other endorses and carries it through without adequate discussion or group consideration. Has high commitment for the two who made it, but generally not for others.
- *Clique*: Similar to the handclasp, but with more people involved. This type usually occurs when a close subgroup decides what is good for the rest of the group. Repeated clique decisions cause splintering of the group and low commitment.

- *Baiting*: A technique that reduces discussion around decisions. A person will say, "Now we are all agreed, right?" and only the very brave will speak up. This usually suppresses obvious dissension and lowers group commitment.
- *Majority rule*: A popular way of making decisions. However, if the outcome of a secret ballot would produce any surprises, it is not a good time to make majority rule decisions. What happens is that a sizable segment of the group may feel devalued and lose their commitment to the decisions on which they "lose" the vote.
- *Consensus*: Similar to Majority Rule, but everyone knows that what they think and value is being considered by all, and there will be no surprises if you vote. Each person will agree that, under the circumstances, the decision made is a fair and workable one and they can live with it and support it.

You may be able to think of and classify other types of decisions. Any type may prove effective under a given set of circumstances. However, it is obvious that the first five approaches are likely to reinforce the powerful in the group and create tension. Morale and membership commitment can be lowered if these are the usual practices of the organisational decisions.

Since members possess the essential ingredients for the solution of all disagreements, group decisions should be based on all the members' input. Certainly, if there are decisions that only take a few people to make, it may not be necessary to involve the entire group. We recommend that you consider the following points about the liabilities and assets of consensus decisions.

Assets of Group Consensus Approach

- Greater sum total of knowledge and information.
- Greater number of approaches to a problem.
- Participation in problem solving increases acceptance.
- Better comprehension of the decision. The chances for communication failures are greatly reduced when the individuals who must work together in executing the decision have participated in making it.

Liabilities of Group Consensus Approach

- *Social pressure*: It has been shown that minority opinions in leaderless groups have little influence on the solution reached even when these opinions are correct ones. Reaching agreement in a group often is confused with finding the "right answer."
- *Individual domination:* Skilled manipulators or dominant individuals can emerge and capture more than their share of influence on the outcome.
- *Conflicting secondary goal:* People may aim at winning the argument at the cost of a best answer.
- *Risk taking:* The risk of not getting their own way can prevent people from fully participating in the discussion.

Group Consensus Guidelines

Effectiveness in communication is of paramount importance in the consensus decision making process. You can enhance your group communication by paying attention to the following 'do's and don'ts."

Do

- Listen not only to the words, but to the rationale being offered.
- Pursue your point and be persistent if you have good information.
- Manage your time effectively, relative to the number of decisions that are being made.
- Involve all team members to ensure use of their knowledge and experience.
- Strive for the best answer. Thinking in cause-and-effect terms avoids dealing only with symptoms.

Don't

- Don't argue for the sake of winning your point. You may learn something by being open-minded.
- Don't give up on your conclusion simply to avoid conflict. Let objective reasons or sound information prevail.
- Don't allow the group to get hung up on a specific item. Move on and come back later.
- Don't compete by assuming that someone must win and someone must lose. Look for the best alternative.
- Don't resort to voting. This tends to split the group into winners and losers.

Leader's Role

This approach to group decision making places the leader in a particular role in which he/she must cease to contribute, avoid evaluation, and refrain from thinking about solutions or group products. Instead he/she must concentrate on the group process by assuming responsibility for accurate communication among members.

The way decisions are made testify to the degree of effectiveness of a group. Here is a list of facts about effective and ineffective groups:

Effective Groups

- Generate more ideas than individuals.
- Have a high level of participation.
- Develop a climate where members can be relaxed, open and direct.
- Are task oriented.

Ineffective Groups

- Pool ignorance and misinformation.
- Eject non-conforming members.
- Force members to comply or compromise.
- Engage in group-think.
- Take action because they cannot think of any reason not to.

Effective Group Members

- Defer to members who they are certain have the facts.
- Form loyalties to their own group.
- Encourage and support other group members.
- Mediate differences in the group.

Ineffective Group Members

- Give in on items they are sure of.
- Oppose or block decisions without cause.
- Dominate discussions.

By following these tips concerning group work and achieving consensus, your group can avoid the negative aspects and enjoy the reward of knowing your group has done its best to achieve a true consensus.

In the next section, we discusss about the orienting of new members:

ORIENTING NEW MEMBERS

Developing and conducting an organisational recruitment campaign is very important. Yet, as we know, retaining these members is another matter entirely. All too frequently groups skip any form of orientation and just place their new recruits directly on committees or organisational projects.

Although involvement is crucial to the longevity of the group, understanding the organisation and its goals and objectives, structure, norms and taboos is equally as important. By taking the time to orient new members to the responsibilities and privileges of membership, the organisation will develop people who can and will make significant contributions. A successful organisational orientation programme should include:

- Organisational history, traditions, and programmes.
- Assimilation of new members into the organisation.
- Rights and responsibilities of members.
- Organisational governance, operating policies and procedures.
- An overview of campus services, activities and programmes for student organisations.
- Information about any support groups or affiliations the group may have.

When planning your orientation programme, keep the word AIM in mind.

- Acquaint.
- Inform.
- Motivate.

Acquaint: The purpose of any orientation programme is to acquaint your recruits to both the organisation and to each other. Knowing the in's and out's of the group is only one aspect of being in an organisation. It is important to note that people join groups for many different reasons such as:

- Wanting to get involved.
- Learning new skills
- Making friends.
- Having a good time.

Therefore, it is important to structure time for the membership to get to know each other and develop personal relationships. Get acquainted exercises that are helpful are

- Pairing off with someone you do not know.
- Write down ten words or phrases that describe yourself.
- Take five minutes to tell your partner about yourself.
- After you have talked to your partner, write down five words or phrases to describe him/her.
- Swap lists and compare yours with the one your partner made of you.
- Gather into a group of six or more and introduce your partner to the rest of the group. Try to include as much information as you can recall.

Officers should be included in the exercise. When all the groups have finished, have the officers take time to tell the entire group about themselves; be sure they include their job descriptions.

Informing your members should include the organisation's history, purpose and structure. If there are written records, be sure to give everyone a copy. In addition, include organisational charts, officer descriptions and a complete membership list. If you do not have a written history, have the group write one. The following will be helpful in starting this project:

- Place newsprint on the wall and select a recorder.
- Ask membership to tell what they know about the organisation.
    - How the group was formed.
    - When and where it started.
    - What past members were like.
    - Programmes and/or services they offered.
    - How the organisation was structured.
    - How the organisation has evolved over the years.
- When recording this information, utilise your creativity and think up interesting chapter titles.

It is important to remember that this is an oral history and that you are recording people's perceptions about the group. Although these may be inaccurate, they are important because they influence people's feelings about the group. This collective writing of your group's history also provides the leadership with the opportunity to dispel myths and rumours.

Motivate your members and get them excited about the group. Provide time for "older" members to meet the new recruits and share ideas and expectations. Below is a good exercise for both your old and new members. Have the group break into groups of old and new members to discuss the following:

- **Outgoing Members**
    - What accomplishments are you most proud of?
    - What advice would you offer to new members?
    - If you had your year to do over again, how would you do it differently?
- **New Members**
    - What would you like this organisation to mean to you one year from now?
    - What would you like to ask the old members?
    - What goals would you like to accomplish this year?
    - What problems do you anticipate and how would you solve them?

Spend at least 15 minutes in your group discussing these questions. When time is up, gather together as one group and report what you discussed. It is often most effective to have the outgoing members report first, followed by the new members.

Finally, it is important to find out what the new members' interests are and what skills they bring to the group. Using this information, try to give them tasks which will successfully use their talents. Further, give them a reason to be committed. Whenever possible, recognise members' accomplishments, both publicly and privately. If they report to a committee chair, be sure to let their superiors know about their contributions.

By including the above suggestions in your new members' orientation programme, you will discover that you have built group cohesion. By following these tips you will ensure:

- New members know the organisation and are able to articulate its purpose.
- Members understand their rights and responsibilities to self and organisation.
- Leadership and discipline.

4

BUILDING A WINNING TEAM

The team-building process is something you will be able to talk over with your coach before you put it into practice in the real world. The basic stages involved are to clarify the goals of the team, identify any issues which may inhibit the team from achieving their goals, and then to address those issues to enable the team to be successful. The essential skills you need are the ability to recognise the right issues, and the ability to resolve them in an appropriate way. Your coach will be able to provide objective guidance and feedback at every stage, and to share in your, and your team's, ultimate success!

TEAM-BUILDING: IDEAS AND ISSUES

Executive Team

Team building can mean different things to different people, and can take a different form depending on the size and nature of the team. An ideal team may consist of a group of people who are committed to achieving a common objective, produce high quality results, who work well together and enjoy their work.

Team members should be valued and have a sense of belonging. People should feel a sense of worth and involvement, where their ideas are heard and their contribution is recognised. They should be given worthwhile tasks and clearly understand what is expected of them. Individuals should be given challenge and responsibility that contribute to the team's objectives and match their abilities. Most importantly, they should have confidence in the leadership, based on consistent fairness and support backed with recognition when it is due.

Of course individual group members also have a responsibility to the team, to participate fully and effectively and to support the goals and efforts of the group as a whole.

International quality consultant and author Peter Scholtes suggests the following five key issues to be considered in team building:

- *Interdependence*: Each member's outcomes are partially determined by the other members of the team.
- *Goal specification*: It is important for the team to have shared goals and to communicate about these.
- *Cohesiveness*: The extent to which team members' skills and abilities mesh together to enable them to perform.
- *Roles and norms*: Every team develops a set of rules (norms) governing their behaviour and also has a number of different roles so that the team can perform the task.
- *Communication:* Listening, giving feedback and having an effective communication network are all vital for team performance.

Improve Teamwork

In the end we discuss, how we improve teamwork.

The foundation of good teamwork is having a shared commitment to common objectives. Without this, all other forms of team building will have a limited impact. Therefore, before using any team building exercises and activities, or looking at relationships in the team, or embarking on other forms of team building, you need to put this foundation of shared commitment in place by:

- Clarifying the team goals, and building ownership/ commitment to those goals across the team.
- Identifying any issues which inhibit the team from reaching their goals, randemoving the inhibitors.
- Putting in place enablers to help the goals be achieved to higher standards.
- Using team processes in the correct sequence to help the team climb one rung at a time up the ladder of performance.

Team building is therefore not just a single event (though events can play a part), nor is it something that can be done by someone outside the team (though outside consultants can help). It is a task primarily for the team manager and the team members themselves.

Types of Team Building

Once you have established the basic foundation of shared commitment, the approach you then take to team building depends on the size of the team and the types of issues that may be inhibiting good teamwork.

Individuals

In a project environment, where team composition is continually changing, the emphasis must be on selecting people who are self-starters and developing the skills in individuals to become effective team members very quickly. The 'scale' involved is one person, and the team building consultant or trainer is endeavouring to change the skills and abilities of the individual at operating within a team.

Small teams

In teams where membership is static—typically in management teams—the motivational challenge is to align the drive of the disparate individuals around the same goals. There can be many inhibitors to performance —e.g.: personality, dynamics, processes etc., and how the individuals within the team relate to each other can have a big bearing on team performance. So, if a member leaves, or another joins, the dynamics of the team can be changed greatly and the task of team building has to start again. Here, the scale is small—say, 2 to about 12—and the main priorities are to build the foundation of collective ownership of team objectives, and then overcome inhibitors through team bonding, facilitation, processes, etc.

Team Islands

A larger scale operates between teams. Where the teams do not relate well, they are called 'team islands'. The motivational challenge is to overcome the problem of "in/out groups" so that people have positive attitudes towards those in other teams. There are often many barriers between teams that inhibit team performance, but not all of them can be removed. The main task, therefore, is the bridging, or relationship, between the teams.

Large teams

The largest scale is organisational culture change. With the exception of the senior management team, any changes to personnel have limited impact on the corporate culture. The key aim of company-wide team-building is to change the behaviours and attitudes prevalent in the organisation, which are almost independent of who actually works there—new recruits.

Corporate Events and Social Responsibility

Also consider the effects of team building and corporate events in terms of effects on employees' families and people's broader life needs. It is easy to become very narrowly focused on the organisation and the community within it, without thinking of the families and social needs outside. Alcohol is another increasing area of risk for organisers of team building and conference events.

An employer's duty of care (and potential liability) at corporate events traditionally was fulfilled by ensuring no-one tripped over the electrical cable for the overhead projector. Nowadays organisations have a deeper wider responsibility, which is progressively reflected in law. Alcohol and discrimination are big issues obviously, but arguably a bigger responsibility for employers is to the families and social well-being of employees, which impacts directly onto society as a whole.

Today's well-led and ethically-managed corporations understand that divisive treatment of employees' partners and families undermines loyalty and motivation of employees, and creates additional unnecessary stresses for workers in close loving caring relationships, especially for young families, which have evolved a strong sensitivity to such pressures.

If you read about Erik Erikson's Life Stages Theory you will understand why parents of young children especially are not helped by this sort of work pressure. Thwarting or obstructing people's instincts—evolved over millennia—to be with and take care of their partners and young families is extremely destructive. Employers who have a blatant antipathy for these crucial life needs of their people are therefore socially irresponsible.

Inevitably strong work commitments put pressure on employees' families and partners. This is particularly so in big modern corporations where travel and lengthy absence from home is unavoidable in key roles. Modern ethical socially responsible organisations should be doing whatever they can to minimise these effects, not make them worse.

Where possible employers should reward partners and families for their support and loyalty, rather than alienate them by creating selfish staff-only events.

Laws are not yet clearly defined about the employer's liabilities arising from such situations, however there are clear principles (e.g., related to stress, duty of care, social responsibility, etc) which demand responsibility and anticipation from employers in this area.

Moreover, fostering a healthy work and home life balance tends to make organisations run smoother and less problematically, notably in areas of grievance and counselling, stress and conflict, disputes and litigation, recruitment and staff retention, succession planning, company reputation and image.

IDEAS FOR TEAM BUILDING

There are many different types of team building activities that you can consider doing in your team, falling into the categories of:

- Outdoor/Indoor Pursuits.
- Workshops.
- Social Events.
- Community Service or Charitable Work.
- Changes to Work Practices.

— Individual Training/Development.

Outdoor/indoor Pursuits

There are a wide variety of pursuits available, from conventional ones such as canoeing or rock climbing, to more unusual ones, such as blind-four-wheel-driving or sheep-driving. We can't list them all here, because there are so many, but there is a selection on our outdoor team building activities page. These pursuits are often expensive.

If physical activity is a problem for some members of the group, then there are some outdoor pursuits that are less active, such as:

— treasure hunt.

— making a video.

— hot air ballooning.

— cooking etc.

If those are too active, you could then try indoor pursuits, such as:

— 10-pin bowling.

— Quasar.

— Casino games etc.

Workshops

Workshops enables a group to focus on a particular topic without interruption.

In many situations, the most effective type of workshop is one that involves everyone in forming collective goals or developing strategic or tactical plans. This engenders ownership amongst all members, and is one of the most powerful team building activities you can use.

Other types of workshops can help to develop better relationships, mutual understanding or solve particular business issues:

- Group games and exercises (that have learning points).
- Psychometrics or personality questionnaires (to develop better interpersonal understanding).
- Business problem solving, or information exchange.
- Customer interaction forums (eg: ask customers to provide feedback on the service, or what they want from you in the future.
- Technology exchange (invite leading figures from the industry to present their vision of the future).

Social Events

These are often the most cost-effective form of team building activities, because they are low cost and high impact. It is often important to make sure that people mix, especially with larger groups, otherwise people just stick with their friends. Here are some ideas for social events:

- Lunch-time drink.
- Evening meal/BBQ.
- Family picnic.
- Quiz nights etc.

Social events can be organised for very little cost and are like the oil in an engine: they can help keep the heat down and things running smoothly.

Charitable Work

Why not choose to do something that has a benefit to the community? Achieving something worthwhile can help to unite the group even more, providing it is not too difficult a task and does not create too much pressure.

Changes to Work Practices

Having a day offsite or doing something that is fun may have a short term impact, but to improve communication, co-operation, etc. in the long-term, you may need to introduce new work practices, such as:

- Team meetings/Cascade briefings.
- Job swapping.
- Team newsletter (for larger teams).
- Open door policy.
- MBWA (Management By Walk About), for all staff, not just management.

Training and Development

It can be beneficial to combine team building activities with individual training. That is, the group receives training, but does so as a group. This has the dual benefit of developing the individuals whilst going through the experience collectively. Such courses could include:

- Communications.
- Persuasion.
- Negotiation.
- Technical training etc.

DEVELOPING SUCCESSFUL TEAMS IN ORGANISATIONS

Over twenty years ago, automobile manufacturers Volvo and Toyota implemented team-based structures at a time when highly formalised, centralised and departmentalised mechanistic structures were the norm. In the 1980s, a growing number of private and public sector organisations began to introduce teams. In the 1990s, the utilisation of teams has spread rapidly. Small manufacturing firms such as the Toowoomba Foundry believe that the development of strong and effective production and managerial teams will lead to the potential for higher performance and increased job satisfaction. Larger firms such as Reliance are encouraging the development of teams, where appropriate, across all aspects of their operations because they believe that there are synergies to be gained from greater levels of involvement in the workforce. It seems that the utilisation of teams has spread to the point that it is now the bureaucratic and mechanistic organisational designs that are becoming the exception rather than the norm.

While the use of teams appears to offer many benefits, teams may not be the most suitable approach for all organisations. This Chapter attempts to outline some of the attractions and challenges of implementing teams so as to give a realistic preview of what can be achieved through teamwork. It should be noted that not all organisations would experience all of the challenges. The effects of teamwork are contingent upon many factors, including the organisation's culture and climate, effectiveness of team leadership, organisational support and so on.

Attraction of Teamwork

The attraction of teamwork stems from the reasons teams are implemented. A number of authors state that teams are being implemented in ever-increasing numbers as a reaction to increased global competition. While increased competitiveness may be occurring, it also seems that there is a growing need to cater for niche markets. Not only must manufacturers and service providers compete on cost, they must also compete on innovation by creating unique products and services that cannot be rivalled by other companies. This creates a problem where companies can no longer rely on mass production and economies of scale to compete in the marketplace.

Many companies believe that teams are the answer to this problem. Teams can maximise organisational innovation because employees have increased autonomy, increased participation, and ownership regarding decisions. The employees are no longer told what to do. Instead, they are given goals, or they develop goals with their team leader, and are then free to decide how best to achieve the goals. In addition to maximising innovation, teams can provide a number of other attractions for the organisations in which they operate.

First, teams make optimum use of human resources as they allow organisations to gain access to an individual's knowledge and skills. The increasing complexity of organisations means that managers can no longer know everything about every aspect of the organisation's operations. In this situation it is essential that the knowledge and skills of the workforce be utilised. Second, teams enhance organisational learning because employees are able to experiment and create strategies that are best suited to their work. Third, teams can result in gains in an individual's productivity and efficiency, thereby creating a synergy. Finally, team work is associated with a greater variety of tasks and added responsibility for team members, which is likely to result in increased levels of job satisfaction, motivation and employee commitment. This may result in lower staff turnover and absenteeism, thereby reducing organisational costs and improving an organisation's memory or knowledge base.

Implementation of Teams

The implementation of teams is, fundamentally, an

organisational change and development process. Teams are, therefore, susceptible to all the challenges that can occur during any organisational change process. In particular, employee resistance may result where employees are required to work with other employees with whom they are unfamiliar. In this case, the new teams are breaking up established social relationships. One way in which this can be overcome is through team building. Team-building attempts to 'improve group performance by improving communication, reducing conflict, and generating greater cohesion and commitment among work group members'. Employee resistance may also result for other reasons. For example, teamwork may require job enlargement. This often occurs when individuals are required to perform their conventional roles as well as their team duties. In this situation, it may be necessary to either reduce some of their duties or to change the system of compensation and rewards.

Along with job enlargement, teamwork is often associated with empowerment, ownership and added responsibility. Managers often assume that individuals prefer to be involved in decision making, rather than simply being told what to do. While this may be true in most cases, it is not true in all cases. This may result in alienation for some employees, which may then lead to job dissatisfaction, labour turnover and/or decreased performance. While there is no simple remedy for this problem, training or a change of position within the organisation may be possible. Another problem associated with 'empowered' teams occurs when the teams are not trusted enough to make major decisions. As a result, teams and the organisation to which they belong, are not reaching their full potential. Where teams are required to seek permission before implementing ideas, timeliness and ownership are reduced. Innovation is also reduced as teams are forced to suggest solutions that are likely to be accepted. Furthermore, team members may believe that management is merely paying lip service to the fundamental ideas of teamwork. This will almost certainly reduce employee morale.

Where teams are trusted to make decisions it may be found that they take up more time than the system they replaced. This is also likely where coordination is required and where a number of teams are interdependent. The problem may be partly overcome by team building, but is likely to required continued training and development of team members. Such training will be particularly relevant for new staff, as there may not be set procedures for them to follow. Coordination also requires effective team leadership. Put simply, efficient team performance requires:

> "a balance between autonomy and decentralisation of power on the one hand, for the sake of both motivation and flexibility, and centralised control on the other hand, for the sake of coordination and predicability".

As is the case with all organisational change and development initiatives, the organisational culture and climate needs to be considered. It should not be assumed that the goals and values of employees are the same as the goals of management, or even that goals and values are consistent across the organisation. Employee attitudes concerning teams will determine the likelihood of success. For teams to be implemented successfully, they need to be an extension of existing values. However, the implementation of teamwork may also be useful where a culture change is desirable. Teamwork demands such a shift in attitudes that organisations may turn to it when they want to achieve a cultural transformation, for example, when becoming customer or quality oriented.

DEVELOPING SUCCESSFUL TEAMS

Although a more comprehensive model for team development proposes eight key points that can facilitate the successful implementation of teams. These points, which embrace both critical elements of teams, as well as enabling factors, are presented below:

1. Clear goals.
2. Decision making authority.
3. Accountability and responsibility.
4. Effective leadership.
5. Training and development.
6. Resources.
7. Organisational support.
8. Rewards for team success.

Clear Goals

Goals should be specific enough to give the team direction. For example, to raise market share by ten percent in six months provides more guidance than simply to raise market share. A goal should also state the ends, rather than the means. This gives teams the freedom to work out how best to achieve the goal. Associated with providing clear goals is the development of meaningful and acceptable performance measures so that the team members can feel confident in their own achievements.

Decision-making Authority

Teams require decision-making authority and, therefore, a certain level of empowerment in order to carry out their work efficiently. Without this authority they would need to get approval for their ideas and these ideas may be rejected before they are either proven or not proven.

For innovation to occur, teams must be allowed to experiment. However, to avoid costly mistakes, it is appropriate to give teams this authority within certain boundaries. It may also be necessary to hand over authority on a gradual basis so team members are not overwhelmed by their newly-acquired authority. People are able to empower themselves through a clear focus and the removal of the sense of fear in what they do.

Accountability and Responsibility

If teams are to enjoy decision making authority, they must also be prepared to be accountable and responsible for their actions. This does not suggest that some failures are not permitted. It does suggest that teams need to monitor customer expectations and also their own performance. If their goals are not being met or customer expectations are not being satisfied, then their approach and methods will need some adjustment.

The acceptance of accountability and responsibility is also associated with the establishment of a positive and productive set of group norms. Work teams can behave similarly to adults in a family environment by developing norms that improve cohesion of the group. Such norms may include sensibility, responsibility, supporting each other, and having fun.

Effective Leadership

Managers and supervisors who become team leaders experience a significant change of role. Team leaders do not direct or control work, but instead work as coaches and mentors. Effective communication, leadership and consulting skills will be required which may necessitate training and development. A new mindset is also required. Team leaders concerned with a loss of power need to understand that their new role is pertinent to the success of the teams, and that their knowledge is required now more than ever. The issue is not about the erosion of power, but a shift in the source of power—from legitimate to knowledge based.

Training and Development

Employees may need to learn new skills such as budgeting, computing, public relations and marketing, as well as skills which allow them to work together effectively, such as effective communication, confliction resolution and problem solving. Training and development are enabling factors that allow team members and leaders to take on new responsibilities. Where team members possess inadequate work skills and knowledge, teams are less likely to succeed.

Resources

For teams to operate effectively they must have access to resources. These resources can include money, time, equipment, technology, people and information. Provision of resources requires trust on the part of the organisation and responsibility on the part of the team members. Like authority, resources should not, and cannot, be unlimited and should perhaps be given to employees gradually.

Organisational Support

Teams cannot operate without the support and commitment of middle and upper management. Therefore, changes must be initiated by those from the top of the organisational hierarchy, rather than those on the shop floor. Any improvements that result from a shop floor initiative may be seen as management incompetence and are not likely to be supported by management. A nurturing environment with a collaborative climate provides the support and encouragement that teams need for job performance.

Rewards for Team Success

An emphasis on individual rewards undermines the effectiveness of team-based work and encourages team members to strive for individual performance goals that may not be congruent with the goals of the team. A team-based reward system should reward employees for teamwork and contributions to team success. One example of such a system is a gainsharing plan whereby ideas that are successful and profitable result in the entire team being rewarded. A problem that may occur with team-based rewards is the problem of social loafing. This occurs when the efforts of one or more members of the team decreases and is more likely to occur in teams that are excessively large. Where team-based rewards are used, social loafers are rewarded similarly to other team members who are responsible for the group performance. This is not an argument for a reward system based on individual efforts, but rather an argument for the necessity of team-based discipline to accompany the team-based reward system.

RESPONSIBILITIES OF TEAM LEADER

- Assign clear tasks to each member.
- Regularly review and monitor progress of work.
- Ensure that the team meets deadlines.
- Discuss and agree on the timetable for major activities with the team.
- Motivate team members.
- Resolve conflicts.
- Give guidance when needed.
- Helps members to overcome barriers.
- Regularly assess team performance using a checklist.

NORMS OF A TEAM

Norms are acceptable standards of behaviours within a group that are shared by group's members. They tell members what they should or should not do depending on the circumstances. In the work environment the most important norms deal with performance-related process. All members should become familiar with these norms and are expected to follow them. It is a good idea to agree on the norms and include them in the team charter.

Examples of Written Norms

- *Team leadership:* The leader/mediator/facilitator has control over the process, e.g. controls when and how much people speak.
- Communication and interpersonal relationships among team members.

Listen

- Allow one person to speak at a time, and avoid side conversations.
- Don't interrupt when a person is talking unless he/she is diverting from the issue being discussed.
- Before evaluating a member's contribution, others check their assumptions to ensure that they have properly understood.
- Seek first to understand others before you seek to be understood.
- Respect the views of all participants.

Talk

- Everyone participates.
- Each person speaks on his/her own behalf and lets others speak for themselves.

- Each person takes responsibility for his/her actions and results.
- One always has three options: accept it, work on it to make it better, or leave. Don't complain if you're not willing to make it better.
- Speak openly and honestly.
- Say what you mean and mean what you say, but preserve people's self-esteem.
- Members can disagree without fear.
- Give negative feedback appropriately: calmly, timely, privately, using present information, focused on issues and behaviours (not individuals). Disagree with what was said, but not with who said it.
- Give specific positive feedback (recognition) right away in public, but adapted to the receiver.
- Call a time out if you need one.
- Communicate immediately if you think you may not be able to fulfil an agreement.
- If you don't understand something, ask for clarification.
- If you see a problem that others haven't noticed, bring it to someone's attention.
- Clear communication of accountabilities for all work team members.

Meetings

- Clear objectives.
- Meetings must have an agenda.
- Meeting information needs to be circulated to everyone prior to the meeting.

- Use the meeting time and keep the discussion focused on the meetings objective(s).
- Start and end meetings on time.
- Use technological tools such as television or video-conferencing to facilitate the meeting.

TEAM CHARTER

A team charter is a written document that defines the team's mission, objectives, scope of operation, time frame, and consequences.

- *The purpose statement*: Explain why the team is being formed. The purpose statement should align with and support the organisation's vision and mission statements.
- *The objectives*: What the team is expected to achieve, stated in measurable terms.
- *The scope of the team's charter* is to define organisational or operational boundaries within which the team is expected and allowed to operate. It includes information about the resources available to the team to accomplish its objectives. It also speaks about the time commitment expected of team members giving due attention to support required in their place of work in performing their day-to-day responsibilities during this assignment.
- A section describing top management's support and commitment to the team.

TIPS FOR BUILDING A WINNING TEAM

Creating teamwork is a challenging process. Merely referring to a collection of employees as a team doesn't make them one. The first question to ask is, is this a team or a group? Each has a purpose. Typically, a team shares leadership and is interdependent, meaning they depend on each other for information, services or products to achieve a team goal. A leader (manager, supervisor) spearheads a group; members work on their own most of the time with little or no dependence on other members to do their job. There may be a group effort but it is not a team. You can't have the same expectations of a group as you do a team. Determine what you are working with, team or group, and proceed from there.

1. *Lay the foundation before you begin construction:* In my experience, the most successful teams invest time in laying the foundation to create a common framework for everyone. The building blocks are in the team infrastructure and team dynamics. You may get started by addressing the following: What is the purpose of the team; their function in relation to the business goals; the actual team goal? I recently posed these questions to a newly formed team of 17 people and got 17 different perspectives. Don't assume everyone is on the same page until you have the discussion.
2. *Make the team aware of the four stages of development:* Those stages are: forming, storming, norming and performing. Explain that the team will progress and digress depending on multiple variables such as turnover and change. Ask the team which stage of development they see themselves and what needs to occur to move to a higher level.
3. *Take a "team pulse". This can happen in a couple of different ways.* One way is through an initial team survey that generates data on how members perceive team functioning and interactions. A survey will include topics such as commitment, trust, communication, and conflict resolution. Administer the survey at least quarterly to

determine progress and team development priorities. Another way to take a team "pulse" is to have periodic frank discussions about what is working and what is not. Practice regular, informal conversations that keep communication channels open.

4. *Assess:* Identify a tool to assess behaviour work style of each team member. This exercise invariably illuminates each member's style preferences, their team contributions, and gives everyone information to adapt and work together more effectively. For most people this creates an "ah ha" experience that is pivotal in fostering understanding and communication.
5. *Push proactivity:* Don't wait until there is conflict to establish a team charter. A charter, generated by team members, should specify guidelines and behavioural boundaries. This will set expectations and clarify what is acceptable and intolerant behaviour. Make it clear that the charter can always be amended. Be sure everyone has a copy. Review it on a regular basis and go through it carefully with a new team member.
6. *Form common skills:* Be sure everyone has a common skill base for communication, conflict resolution, problem solving, giving and receiving peer feedback. Teams who have these common skill sets are much more productive than teams that don't. Technical expertise is only half of the success quotient.
7. *Examine expectations:* Are the expectations of team members and the leader clearly communicated? This goes beyond job descriptions. For example, what do people expect to get out of working together as a team, i.e., expression, creativity; what can be expected of their contributions?

8. *Acknowledge unique talents and contributions:* Each team member brings value to the team. Point out or showcase various abilities. Take time in a meeting to recognise one or two members. Be sure everyone receives equal recognition.
9. *Build dialogue, extinguish monologue:* Aim toward two-way interaction, exchange of ideas, and developing new insights in regular communication. Invite members to ask about others reasoning or thinking and explain how they think of or see a situation.
10. *Do some team building:* Initially you may consider a series of team sessions that incorporate the suggestions above with team building activities. Once the team is grounded, you may benefit by having quarterly or bi-annual team building sessions. The type of team building you choose, from classroom experiential to rope climbing, needs to match the culture and challenges of the team. There are hundreds of activities that are metaphors for what goes on or doesn't go on, in the team experience. Whatever you choose to do, be certain there will be valuable learning and fun.
11. *Laugh together:* Laughter is a common language the entire team will understand. So legitimise levity among team members and you will likely lessen their stress and build their bond. Create times for people to laugh together and loosen up. This will also stimulate creativity. Consider some of these ideas: start a meeting with a relevant joke or funny story, show a clip of a comedy video tape that pertains to a current challenge.
12. *Celebrate:* Provide a continental breakfast or bring in lunch and celebrate for no special reason than to say thank you to the team. Or identify a theme and

ask people to bring in food to share. Play music and decorate the lunch room. Don't expect employees to gather after work hours. Most people have family obligations and personal commitments.

5

TEAM CHARACTERISTICS

If you lead a team, you know that the journey to high-performance is ongoing. It's the rare team that achieves high-performance and just stays there. In our business life, whether we've managed a team within an organisation, or run our own company, it's been unusual to keep the same team together for longer than a year. Team members come and go, driven by the needs of the organisation and their own career goals. And every time the members of a team changes, the team needs to re-group and re-focus.

Experience has demonstrated that successful teams are empowered to establish some or all of a team's goals, to make decisions about how to achieve these goals, to undertake the tasks required to meet them and to be mutually accountable for their results. There are several characteristics of an effective team. These include:

– *Clear purpose*: The vision, mission, goal or task of the team has been defined and is now accepted by everyone. This is an action plan.

– *Informality*: The climate tends to be informal, comfortable and relaxed. There are no obvious tensions or signs of boredom.

- *Participation*: There is much discussion and everyone is encouraged to participate.
- *Listening:* The members use effective listening techniques such as questioning, paraphrasing and summarising to get out ideas.
- *Civilised disagreement:* If there is disagreement, the team must be comfortable with this and show no signs of avoiding, smoothing over or suppressing conflict.
- *Consensus decisions*: For important decisions, the goal is substantial but not necessarily unanimous agreement through open discussion of everyone's ideas, avoidance of formal voting or easy compromises.
- *Open communication*: Team members feel free to express their feelings on the tasks as well as on the group's operation. There are few hidden agendas. Communication takes place outside of meetings.
- *Clear roles and work assignments*: There are clear expectations about the roles played by each team member. When action is taken, clear assignments are made, accepted and carried out. Work is fairly distributed among team members.
- *Shared leadership:* While the team has a formal leader, leadership functions shift from time to time depending on the circumstances, the needs of the group and the skills of the members. The formal leader models the appropriate behaviour and helps establish positive norms.
- *External relations*: The team spends time developing key outside relationships and mobilising resources, then building credibility with important players in other parts of the organisation.

- *Style diversity*: The team has a broad spectrum of team-player types, including members who emphasize attention to task, goal setting, focus on process and questions about how the team is functioning.
- *Self-assessment:* Periodically, the team stops to examine how well it is functioning and what may be interfering with its effectiveness.

What exactly does a good team look like, and how do we recognise one when we see it?

Maybe character is more than just what a team looks like on the surface.

How does a good team get along? Is a competitive or nurturing environment more important to team performance?

Most experts agree, character is the root of what makes a good team in the first place. It makes sense: characteristics $\rightarrow$ character.

I'm sure anyone who has had to suffer through a boss or co-worker who lacked character can certainly agree.

Aurelius' words ring true for the characteristics of a good team as well.

Good teams are led by people who convey a clear vision of the team's purpose, provide the team with the necessary resources to complete their jobs, and maintain the team's overall character.

There are thousands of questions about what makes a good team, but the true measure of great teams is the process by which they succeed. It's clear that great teams simply perform better; the question is: How?

Though innate talent certainly plays a huge factor in team performance, the best teams are not solely talent driven. Great teams are flexible enough to readily evolve methods that work effectively for each member of the team.

Team performance is sharpened by rapidly evolving methods that work for each team member, despite personality differences, skill sets, and critical thinking skills.

- *Participative leadership:* Creating an interdependence by empowering, freeing up and serving others.
- *Shared responsibility:* Establishing an environment in which all team members feel responsibility as the manager for team performance.
- *Alignment of purpose*: Having a sense of common purpose about why the team exists and the function it serves.
- *High communication*: Creating a climate of trust and open, honest communication.
- *Future focused*: Seeing change as an opportunity for growth.
- *Focused on task*: Keeping meetings and interactions focused on results.
- *Utilising skill*: Applying individual talents and creativity.
- *Rapid response:* Identifying and acting on opportunities.

SHARPEN YOUR TEAM'S PERFORMANCE

Good teams don't just happen, they become good through consistent action and constructive feedback. Feedback that doesn't get bogged down in the realm of vague philosophy or nit-picking.

Business teams happen in the real world; discovering what works and is a process of collaborative learning and then focusing on what works. The results for your business can be amazing.

We want to be in control of our own destinies. But the old hierarchical model of dictating people's thoughts and actions doesn't work in this highly networked yet polarised business world.

The characteristics of a good team that we all enjoy, become liabilities and threats under the thumb of a tyrant. Free thinkers and highly talented and skilled team members don't need the stress or pressure of putting up with a manager breathing down their neck.

Codes of Conduct

Staying consistent within a team setting is about not wavering when hardships occur. Coming up with your team's code of conduct is about setting boundaries about what is acceptable and what is not. This type of team building is not for weaklings.

If you're serious about extracting top notch performance from your team, the code of conduct you agree upon cannot be deviated from. So what are some characteristics of a good team's Code of Conduct? It depends upon you unique objectives, purpose, and values.

According to Jim Collins, discovering a company's core values is about asking the "right questions."

- What can we be best in the world at?
- What are you deeply passionate about?
- What drives your economic engine?

Team building is finding the answers to these same questions, but on a smaller scale. To build an effective team the answers to these questions must mesh in order for you to find alignment in your purpose.

Team members must assign similar value to the core characteristics of a good team and their team's code of conduct.

Trying to force values onto people who don't believe in them is a lesson in futility and frustration—kind of like trying to fit a square peg in a round hole.

Team members, employees, managers and companies thrive within effective systems and culture where people are empowered by their work. Team members want a culture where their unique knowledge, experience, and motivation make a difference for themselves and their team.

People will choose the values that reflect their own, and easily accept a code of conduct that allows them to take personal ownership over their position. They want to be an integral part of the team.

It's simple, if your team or company cannot meet the needs of your people or customers, they will find one that can.

The characteristics of good teams are those of the companies that choose their values and purpose with care and passion. Then they create a culture that holds people accountable for their actions, while at the same time creating a system of empowerment for the team's members.

TASK CHARACTERISTICS

Clear Purpose

There is a plan and a strategy. The team has vision of the future. There is a team mission statement or charter. The team has made distinction between long-term and short-term objectives and there is an action plan for these objectives. The vision, mission, goal or objectives of the team have been defined by everyone and there is a joint commitment to these objectives. The team members have the expertise and are empowered to create the vision, mission, goals and objectives. There is an understanding on how team members' objectives contribute to the whole. Teams draw strength and direction from a deep, shared understanding of common purpose.

Understanding of Roles and Structure

The roles of team members are understood. Team members are clear about what is expected of them as well as clear about the roles of others on the team. Work assignments are evenly distributed between team members. While tasks are distributed, they are not necessarily fixed. Team members take responsibility for tasks willingly and assume responsibility for tasks without being asked or assigned. Team members are willing to work outside of their defined roles in order to help the team. Leadership is shared and the issue of control has been resolved to the team's satisfaction. The team leader makes an effort to give members increasing responsibility. All team members feel they have some control over decisions related to distribution of work. Individual talents are utilised. Assignments are distributed according to the skills of team members yet there is a willingness to give challenges and new opportunities to team members.

Output-Impact

The team "delivers the goods". Projects are formulated and completed according to an agreed schedule. The quality and quantity of team output is high and there is a positive impact on the organisation. Others see the team as a highly productive unit. Team products impact and have a positive affect on productivity of other units. Output adds value to the organisation. Work assignments of team members are completed on time and of a high quality. Team members help each other to overcome obstacles to non-performance.

Using Diversity Effectively

The team has a balance in composition of gender, culture, age and experience. The team actively seeks out and welcomes new members who add to its diversity. The team comprises members with a wide range of skills, knowledge and attitudes. There is a mix of strategic thinkers, specialists, monitors, implementers, networkers, etc. There is not one dominant working style, but if there is this is recognised and efforts made to deal with this in some constructive manner. Team diversity is used to the team's benefit. All views and opinions are encouraged and used to enhance the team output. Team members are conscious of team member differences arising out of diversity and behave in a manner that demonstrates this sensitivity.

Problem Solving and Decision-making

The team strives for decisions that are acceptable to all or most members. Differences in opinion are discussed openly and decisions are usually arrived at through consensus. Team members publicly support team decisions when they have had an opportunity to influence the decision, but it has not gone their way. When making decisions, do team members all contribute data required to make a sound decision? There is enough depth in the team and variety of approaches, skills and knowledge to ensure the best decision. The team takes time to look at all sides of a problem, what is the best solution for all concerned and the cost/benefits. The team distinguishes easily between important and less important decisions, spending more time on the former. The team does not spend an inordinate amount of time on reaching decisions which have little importance or impact on output.

External Relations

The team shares responsibility for and spends time developing key outside relationships, mobilising resources and building credibility with important stakeholders in other parts of the organisation. The team is aware of the key external power brokers and persons in positions that may facilitate the achievement of team goals. The team has built up a solid network of support throughout the organisation. The team has an external relations and communications strategy. The team members devote time to external contacts as an investment for the future rather than simply to solve immediate needs. Others see the team in a positive light. Others frequently complement the team on its activities. The team has a set of mechanisms or procedures (e.g. joint meetings, sharing meeting minutes, joint projects) to facilitate relations with other teams. The team has a good way of providing key stakeholders with information about the team.

Self-assessment

Periodically, the team stops to examine how well it is functioning and what may be interfering with its effectiveness. The team will sometimes call on outside assistance to honestly assess team processes and effectiveness. Reflection on task achievements and team processes are open and honest. All team members participate in such processes. Team members listen to the views of all and consider each contribution seriously and on its merits. Team members seek advice on their own personal performance from others. Team members are ready to offer honest and non-threatening advice on others' performance.

CLIMATE CHARACTERISTICS

Team-member Fulfilment

Team members derive a high level of satisfaction from their role in the team and grow in stature through their membership. They are challenged by their team role and tasks. Their potential is recognised and developed. Team members identify with team success as well as feel pride when other team members are recognised for their achievements.

Participation

All team members feel that they are contributing important added value to the team's output. The team leader encourages participation from all staff. New team members are encouraged and helped to become quickly involved in team process. Team members' views are respected. There is a high level of purposeful discussion. No one is marginalised in decision making. Participation is relevant and focused on the task at hand. Monopolisers are discouraged from controlling discussions.

Open Communication

Team members feel free to express their opinion and feelings. There are few hidden agendas. There is a level of trust allowing for honest, frank and non-threatening exchanges. Team members encourage others to express their views. Team members do not criticise others "behind their backs". Active listening is practised. Members allow each other to complete a presentation or opinion without interruption. Team members are attentive to others comments. Team members use inquiry skills. Constructive feedback is given frequently. Team members practice advocacy skills effectively.

Human Relations

Team members treat each other with respect and caring. There is no bossing, aggressive behaviour and accusatory questioning. Harassment is evident in no form whatsoever. Team members are comfortable and happy in each other's company and are frequently socialising. The work environment is fun and free of unnecessary tensions. All staff enjoys coming to work in the morning. There is a high level of informality. There is neither discrimination towards nor unconstructive criticism of others. A positive and constructive atmosphere prevails in the workplace. Corridor talk is primarily positive, not an opportunity to complain about other team members. Optimism is more prevalent than pessimism. Jealousy does not exist.

Energy and Creativity

Team members gain strength from one another. Collectively, they feel more potent and find team activities renew their vitality. Synergy (the team power goes beyond the sum of its individual members) is evident. The team is creative, imaginative and not afraid to take risks. No idea is considered absurd. Team members do not immediately see the negative side or obstacles to suggestions. Initiative is encouraged. The team leader is not threatened by and indeed encourages experimentation and initiatives in team members. There is a shared excitement and enthusiasm when developing new initiatives. Ideas flow freely, one idea building on another.

Civilised Disagreement

Team members are willing to give and receive constructive and non-aggressive criticism without fear or offence. Team members feel free to express different point of views. Team relationships are discussed openly. The team is adept at working out disagreements in order to solve underlying problems rather than the "quick fix". Differences in opinion are encouraged and lead to imaginative solutions to problems.

Learning

Team members are continually seeking better ways of working together and enjoy learning from each other. Personal development is encouraged. The team stimulates learning opportunities. At the same time as team members learn, the team as a whole learns and influences organisational learning. The team reviews experiences and draws conclusions from them to improve performance. Work time is allocated to learning opportunities. The team leader promotes learning by team members.

CHARACTERISTICS OF A SUCCESSFUL TEAM

Right Team Leader

- A skilful leader helps the team maintain its focus on major issues.
- He or she enhances communication in order to be sure that all the possible solutions are being heard.
- A good leader is masterful with people and team-process skills.
- He or she avoids giving advice, but rather, leads the team from problem identification to a plan of action.

Right Team Goals

Team goals are derived from critical farm problems that influence whether the business will exist in ten or twenty years such as the following:

- 30 percent increase in milk sales.
- Change in management styles from stall barn to milking parlours.
- Sale or transfer of the business.
- Arranging a new partnership for the business.
- Specialisation in milk production only.
- New ventures.
- Managing non-family labour.
- Addressing complex unresolved management problems.

Teams should avoid farm problems that don't require the skills, experience, and judgment of off-farm advisers. This is a misuse of valuable resources and will eventually lead to dissatisfaction and dissolution of the advisory team.

Right Team Members

Team members and team problems should be well matched. As the team sets new goals, the composition of the team should be re-evaluated. Having a crop consultant or veterinarian on an intergenerational farm transfer team is likely to underutilise the crop consultant or veterinarian's abilities. An estate planner or attorney might be a better choice.

Outstanding team members should have unique skills, experiences, and judgement not resident on the farm staff. They should also be team players and believe in the team process. Team members that have cross-purposes or hidden agendas can destroy a team's effectiveness and will have to be removed from the team.

Right Meeting Location

A team meeting is not a committee meeting but a highly creative process that benefits from locations that foster thinking and orderly discussion. Teams should meet in an environment similar to a boardroom, comfortable and away from interruptions and distractions.

Right Solution to Critical Problems and Measuring Outcomes of Actions

Complex problems rarely have simple solutions. Using processes for making decisions can clarify solutions, but solutions often need refinement over time. By frequently tracking progress toward goals and using measuring techniques, the team can monitor the degree of success and evaluate when to intercede. Also, the monitoring process helps advisers see progress and assess their time commitment. Without a measured benefit advisers cannot continue to justify their commitment as team members.

Effective monitoring system for Tracking progress

A well-designed monitoring method will help your team determine when its action plan needs to be improved.

Right Plan of Action

Without a clear action plan the wishes of the team may never be completely implemented. Action plans can be simple but should be in writing so the staff implementing the plan can know what is expected, what is being measured, when results are expected, and refer back to it over time. The action plan becomes the beacon for the team.

Communication

Ongoing communication is important between meetings as well as during team meetings.

Regular Evaluation of the team's Performance

Stepping back and asking, "Could we do our team work

better?" is a good start toward evaluating your team's performance.

Celebration of Successes

It is important that you all step back from time to time and acknowledge your progress and celebrate your successes, both small and large.

CHARACTERISTICS OF A HIGH-PERFORMING TEAM

What's a team leader to do? For starters, focus on the seven characteristics of a high-performing team:

- Shared Purpose and Direction.
- Motivating Goals.
- Commitment to Individual and Team Roles.
- Multi-directional Communication.
- Authority to Decide or Act.
- Reliance on Diverse Talents.
- Mutual Support and Trust.

Shared Purpose and Direction

On a high-performing team, everyone on the team is committed to the team's purpose. They know exactly what that purpose is because the team leader keeps them focused by constantly communicating that purpose in team meetings and regular updates. The team leader helps each individual team member meet his or new own needs while serving the overall purpose of the team.

Motivating Goals

The team leader ensures that everyone on the team has clearly defined goals and targets. In some organisations, the strategic goals and departmental objectives are determined by senior management. In that case, the team leader makes sure that these goals are clearly discussed. Team members should understand how their jobs support the achievement of the defined goals, and, if possible, have the opportunity to develop individual goals and action plans that spell out how they will contribute to the success of the organisation.

Commitment to Individual and Team Roles

On a Total Team, team members have clearly defined expectations but they also understand how each of their roles is linked to every other role. Team leaders ensure that team members are cross-trained in other responsibilities so that everyone can back each other up when needed. The team leader makes sure that individual job responsibilities are fulfilled, but, at the same time, works to help the individuals develop a common language, processes and approaches that allow them to function as a team.

Multi-directional Communication

On the best teams, team members solve problems, communicate with each other, and keep the team leader updated on current challenges or emerging issues. On low-performing teams, communication is one-way (from team leader to team members) or two-way (between the team leader and individuals). Skilled leaders focus on developing multi-directional communication, avoiding the trap of communicating with individuals members of the team.

Authority to Decide or Act

No doubt about it, new teams may have to earn this authority by demonstrating that they understand the team's purpose, processes and priorities. However, effective team leaders work toward pushing authority for the team's outcomes to the team members. Team members know how and when to get approval for decisions and, in the best of cases, are charged with making on-the-spot decisions when a customer is facing them. On low-performing teams, team members have to constantly get approval before taking action, significantly reducing their effectiveness and negatively affecting their sense of engagement on the team.

Reliance on Diverse Talents

Savvy team leaders pay attention to helping team members understand their unique strengths, talents, and weaknesses. No individual team member can be good at everything. The best team leaders assist everyone to develop an appreciation for individual style differences, natural gifts, and personal experience. Teams are encouraged to use the language of acceptance and appreciation, rather than criticism and judgement. Team leaders consciously hire team members who bring complementary skill sets, unique experience, and diverse perspectives.

Mutual Support and Trust

The seventh characteristic may be the most important, and frankly, is probably the most elusive. The team leader can't force a team to be supportive and trusting-it's a natural result of shared responsibility, shared success, and mutual respect. The high-performing team achieves mutual support and trust because they have a history of working together to achieve grand dreams and results. They have met challenges, overcome obstacles, backed each other up in good times and bad. The Total Team has earned each other's trust.

SUM UP

Building a high-performing team is not an easy task. However, if you're a team leader that is up to the challenge, then consciously focus on developing these seven characteristics. Bring them to your next team meeting and ask team members to evaluate them. How do you know whether each of these characteristics is present or absent on your team? What is the team willing to do to develop these seven characteristics? Then ask the individuals on your team to commit to 3-5 specific actions they will take in the next 60 days.

6

UNDERSTANDING TEAM ROLES

When a team is performing at its best, you'll usually find that each team member has clear responsibilities. Just as importantly, you'll normally see that every role needed to achieve the team's goal is being performed fully and well.

But often, despite clear roles and responsibilities, a team will fall short of its full potential. How often does this happen in the teams you work with? Perhaps some team members don't complete what you expect them to do. Perhaps some team members are not quite flexible enough, so things 'fall between the cracks'. Maybe someone who is valued for their expert input fails to see the wider picture, and so misses out tasks or steps that others would expect. Or perhaps one team member become frustrated because he or she disagrees with the approach of another team members.

BELBIN TEAM ROLES MODEL

The Belbin Team Roles method, also referred to as Belbin Team Inventory, was developed by Dr. Raymond Meredith Belbin and first published in his 1981 book Management Teams. It is a model that can be used to describe and gain insight into the behavior of one team member in relationship to another. The Belbin Team Role

Inventory assesses how an individual behaves in a team environment. It is therefore a behavioural tool, subject to change, and not a psychometric instrument. Belbin suggests that, by understanding your team role within a particular team, you can develop your strengths and manage your weaknesses as a team member, and so improve how you contribute to the team. Team leaders and team development practitioners often use the Belbin model to help create more balanced teams. Teams can become unbalanced if all team members have similar styles of behaviour or team roles.

If team members have similar weakness, the team as a whole may tend to have that weakness. If team members have similar team-work strengths, they may tend to compete for the team tasks and responsibilities that best suit their natural styles. So you can use the model with your team to help ensure that necessary team roles are covered, and that potential behavioural tensions or weaknesses among the team member are addressed.

Belbin identified nine team roles and he categorised those roles into three groups:

1. Action Oriented,
2. People Oriented, and
3. Thought Oriented.

Each team role is associated with typical behavioural and interpersonal strengths. Belbin also defined characteristic weaknesses that tend to accompany the team-role. He called the characteristic weaknesses of team-roles the "allowable" weaknesses; as for any behavioural weakness, these are areas to be aware of and potentially improve. The nine team-roles are:

Action Oriented Roles

Shapers

Shapers are people who challenge the team to improve.

They are dynamic and usually extroverted people who enjoy stimulating others, questioning norms, and finding the best approaches to problems. The Shaper is the one who shakes things up to make sure that all possibilities are considered and that the team does not become complacent. Shapers often see obstacles as exciting challenges and they tend to have the courage to push on when others feel like quitting. Their potential weaknesses may be that they're argumentative, and that they may offend people's feelings.

Implementer

Implementers are the people who get things done. They turn the team's ideas and concepts into practical actions and plans. They are typically conservative, disciplined people who work systematically and efficiently and are very well organised. These are the people who you can count on to get the job done. On the downside, Implementers may be inflexible and somewhat resistant to change.

Completer-Finisher

Completer-Finishers are the people who see that projects are completed thoroughly. They ensure there have been no errors or omissions and they pay attention to the smallest of details. They are very concerned with deadlines and will push the team to make sure the job is completed on time. They are described as perfectionists who are orderly, conscientious, and anxious.

However, a Completer-Finisher may worry unnecessarily and find it hard to delegate.

People Oriented Roles

Coordinator

Coordinators are the ones who take on the traditional team-leader role and have also been referred to as the chairmen. They guide the team to what they perceive are the objectives. They are often excellent listeners and they are naturally able to recognise the value that each team members brings to the table. They are calm and good-natured and delegate tasks very effectively. Their potential weaknesses are that they may delegate away too much personal responsibility, and may tend to be manipulative.

Team Worker

Team Workers are the people who provide support and make sure the team is working together. These people fill the role of negotiators within the team and they are flexible, diplomatic, and perceptive. These tend to be popular people who are very capable in their own right but who prioritise team cohesion and helping people getting along. Their weaknesses may be a tendency to be indecisive, and maintain uncommitted positions during discussions and decision-making.

Resource Investigator

Resource Investigators are innovative and curious. They explore available options, develop contacts, and negotiate for resources on behalf of the team. They are enthusiastic team members, who identify and work with external stakeholders to help the team accomplish its objective. They are outgoing and are often extroverted, meaning that others are often receptive to them and their ideas. On the downside, they may lose enthusiasm quickly, and are often overly optimistic.

Thought Oriented Roles

Plant

The Plant is the creative innovator who comes up with new ideas and approaches. They thrive on praise but criticism is especially hard for them to deal with. Plants are often introverted and prefer to work apart from the team. Because their ideas are so novel, they can be impractical at times. They may also be poor communicators and can tend to ignore given parameters and constraints.

Monitor-Evaluator

Monitor-Evaluators are best at analysing and evaluating ideas that other people (often Plants) come up with. These people are shrewd and objective and they carefully weigh the pros and cons of all the options before coming to a decision. Monitor-Evaluators are critical thinkers and very strategic in their approach. They are often perceived as detached or unemotional. Sometimes they are poor motivators who react to events rather than instigating them

Specialist

Specialists are people who have specialised knowledge that is needed to get the job done. They pride themselves on their skills and abilities, and they work to maintain their professional status. Their job within the team is to be an expert in the area, and they commit themselves fully to their field of expertise. This may limit their contribution, and lead to a preoccupation with technicalities at the expense of the bigger picture.

How to Use Belbin Team Roles Model

The Belbin Team Roles Model can be used in several ways: You can use it to think about team balance before a project starts, you can use it to highlight and so manage interpersonal differences within an existing team, and you can use it to develop yourself as a team player.

The tool below helps you analyse team membership, using the Belbin team roles as checks for potential strengths and weakness. Use Belbin's model to analyse your team, and as a guide as you develop your team's strengths, and manage its weaknesses:

1. Over a period of time, observe the individual members of your team, and see how they behave, contribute and behave within the team.
2. Now list the members of the team, and for each person write down the key strengths and characteristics you have observed.
3. Compare each person's listed strengths and weakness with the Belbin's descriptions of team-roles, and note the one that most accurately describes that person.
4. Once you have done this for each team member, consider the following questions:
    - Which team roles are missing from your team? And from this, ask yourself which strengths are likely to be missing from the team overall?
    - Is there are prevalent team role that many of the team members share?
5. Once you have identified potential weakness, areas of conflict and missing strengths, consider the options you have to improve and change this.

Consider:

- Whether an existing team member could compensate by purposefully adopting different a team role. With awareness and intention, this is sometimes possible.
- Whether one or more team members could improve how they work together and with others to avoid potential conflict of their natural styles.
- Whether new skills need to brought onto the team to cover weaknesses.

TASK AND PROCESS ROLES

When involved in teamwork people usually take on one or more typical roles. Task roles help the group achieve its aims and goals. Process roles help the group to remain focused and harmonious. Group members usually take more than one role or play different roles in different groups. Some task and process roles. When involved in teamwork people usually take on one or more typical roles. Task roles help the group achieve its aims and goals. Process roles help the group to remain focused and harmonious. Group members usually take more than one role or play different roles in different groups. Some task and process roles are outlined in the table below.

Table 6.1: Task and Process Roles

Task roles	*Actions and behaviours*
Starts the group working	Initiates action by proposing goals and tasks.
Suggests directions	Develops plans for approaching the task and sharing responsibilities; helps group focus on the task.
Offers information and opinions	Offers facts, opinions, ideas, suggestions and relevant information.
Process roles	*Actions and behaviours*
Listens actively	Welcomes others' ideas while expressing their own; is receptive to others' ideas and gives verbal and non-verbal feedback to the speaker.
Encourages	Warmly encourages participation from all group members, clearly values and accepts contributions.
Compromises and harmonises	Tries to reconcile disagreements when opinions differ or conflict arises.

Team Leader

Some teams select a team member to be the team leader. Other teams decide to rotate the leadership position between team members. Some teams decide to have no team leader and roles and responsibilities for the team are shared or develop as the team progresses.

Groups who select a team leader may nominate the team leader to take responsibility for some team tasks including:

- Acting as spoke-person for the group.
- Planning meeting agendas.
- Obtaining resources.
- Setting meeting times.
- Chairing meetings.

An effective team leader is a team member who initiates actions and assumes team roles which assist the team to reach its goals. The team leader will listen more than talk, summarises discussion and moves the team onto completion of the task.

Team Scribe (or Recorder)

A team will decide to have a scribe or recorder when it is important for teams to have records of:

- What has been discussed.
- What decisions have been made.
- What actions have been decided on.
- Who is responsible for identified actions.

Team Reporter

A team will nominate a reporter who verbally reports back to the whole group or class. A reporter will be required to:

- Accurately summarise what has been discussed.
- Clearly explain what decisions have been made.
- Present effectively.
- Answer questions (perhaps).

When you take on the role of reporting your team's discussion and decisions to the whole class, you also can develop the confidence to present orally in a familiar environment—although you may initially feel somewhat anxious. One strategy which is helpful to allay these anxieties is to ask the scribe to write on an overhead transparency, so that you can use these notes and everyone can view them.

Volunteer for a variety of roles and responsibilities within teams so that you can gain experience and improve your skills.

Values of Team Members

In the last we discuss the values of team members.

A well working team is much greater than the sum of its parts. When working with your project team do you want to:

- Hone your skill as a facilitator.
- Extract the best ideas.
- Invite creativity.
- Protect against members shutting down members.

If you said yes to the above then it is important to create a positive context and establish a high level of cooperation. Every interaction with team members is an opportunity to increase creativity, improve morale and make projects run smoother. How do you make the most of these opportunities? Three tips are given below:

1. Appreciate differences.
2. Validate everyone's contributions.
3. Celebrate.

Appreciate Differences

Team members have work style differences. Some focus mostly on tasks and others focus on interactions with people. Some are methodical and some are quick to act. In spite of these differences some team members work together well and have high levels of productivity. Their differences can cause conflicts yet they are used as fuel for innovation. When appreciating individual differences team members thrive on conflicts.

Focusing on differences between team members as if there is something wrong with the other person has a negative effect on team dynamics and productivity. Encourage team members to take a positive view and find value in how other people see and do things? The most creative and successful project teams are the ones use their differences to compliment and support each other.

Validate everyone's contributions

You grow what you notice and validate. By recognising someone's efforts, pointing out how they are helping the team and the project, you increase those behaviours. Especially if something they are working on is challenging. Find what they are doing that is valuable and point it out. This helps to maintain self esteem and keep morale high. When people receive validation and acknowledgement at work their report of job satisfaction increases.

Celebrate

Celebration lifts spirits and reinforces success. It sparks enthusiasm. Find little things to celebrate everyday. Do not pass up any opportunities to acknowledge what is going right, help team members to bond and raise morale. Some ways to celebrate are getting bonuses, awards, or mention in a meeting. Some times team members share trips, meals, or chocolate. Some time there is applause, congratulations or a high five. Celebration can be done for little or no cost.

7

TEAM COMMUNICATION

Team effectiveness is dependent upon team communication. The quality of the team's work, to a large extent, depends upon the quality of the information shared. The ability of team members to understand and communicate information enables them to work together collaboratively. Creative people, like you and me, want to feel a sense of ownership in our day-to-day work lives. We want to "buy in" to the system and the team within which we work. This "buying in" is initiated by good communication... the way we communicate the ideas, strategies, and frameworks by which we work.

As a leader, effective communication is a matter of getting to know what makes the individuals on our teams tick on a personal level. Then begin the dialogue by establishing a working relationship on that level. Significant time, resources, and energy is required to establish relationships like these on some large corporate teams, but for small business teams, where resources are not always easy to come by, time and energy must make up the difference.

On small teams, the ability to make meaningful personal connections with your fellow team members is easier because you must work closely together to accomplish your goals. Even on small teams the principles of leadership still apply:

– Model the way.

– Inspire a shared vision.

– Challenge the process.

– Enable action.

– Encourage the heart.

These are real principles of good team building and the result of effective team communication skills. By keeping these principles in mind while communicating collectively with your team, or individually with the team members you can develop deeper relationships and more effectively get your employees to "buy in" to your organisational concept.

For us, the shared sense of ownership in the workplace is true empowerment because you feel the swell of pride when you realise your team and organisation truly represents what you stand for individually. Your identity doesn't have to make adjustments for the actions of your organisation.

This concept begins with the words you use individually, at the team level, and an organisational level. Good, effective communication is the key that unlock true organisational performance.

But still, how do we ensure effective communication on our team? And how does our communication impact how people perform?

In a team setting, effective team communication skills come at a huge premium.

Studies have shown, through good communication we can get more done, more effectively, and quicker that when the lines of communication break down.

By making deeper, more meaningful, connections with more people on your team and nurturing those connections is the true beginning of effective team communication skills.

Using these skills you'll inspire more, higher quality work from individual team members, make more connections, and leverage the collective value of your entire team.

With open lines of communication, information will flow back to you like a river because you'll find yourself more connected to the sources of feedback and "centers of influence' within your organisation.

Making these meaningful connections is essential to effective team communication skills for your entire team because by modelling right action, you inspire your team to do the same.

EFFECTIVE COMMUNICATION SKILLS

Effective communication skills empower an individual to inspire and influence others in order to reach the desired outcome, no matter how difficult the situation may appear to be. An individual with effective communication skills not just has an edge over his/her fellow colleagues/ friends/acquaintances etc. but also carries out his/her job with a lot of confidence, ease and perfection. Effective communication skills combined with appropriate body language can help anyone in leaving a mark behind with each interaction he/she has.

Most organisations, now, work on different projects simultaneously with separate teams allocated to each project. Depending on the project size and scope these teams can be small or large. Irrespective of the number of employees in a team, it is essential that every member of a team understands and shares relevant information related to the project. It is also important that they have a clear picture of their roles and responsibilities with respect to the project and deliver accordingly. Thus, in order to ensure a successful project execution, it is important that the team members share a healthy relationship based on trust, confidence and mutual understanding.

Developing effective communication skills within the team can be done easily by imbibing some basic manners, professional etiquettes and keeping an open mind. Having effective team communication skills is a crucial requirement for both leaders and team members alike. It allows you to establish harmonious relationships, fully understand the team's intention, share your ideas easily, and even impress other team members.

Listen Well

Some people end up being poor listeners because they would daydream or think of something else instead of listening attentively to the speaker. Focus on the other party's message instead of thinking in advance on what to say next.

Don't let the speaker's manner of speaking, background or experience, outside appearance, race, religion, etc. distort your judgment in understanding the meaning of the message.

Never speak when the other person is talking. That is plain impolite. Wait a few seconds after the other party stops speaking before you talk. When it's time for you to speak, avoid changing subjects because this indicates your disinterest; this is also a sign of disrespect.

Listening and clearly understanding the other party's messages are the most effective team communication skills; so make sure you listen more than you talk. We're given two ears and one mouth for a good reason.

Speak Clearly and Purposefully

If you didn't understand anything said by a speaker, kindly ask him to repeat or clarify what he said. Always show respect, courtesy and politeness.

Give meaningful feedback and suggestions. Get straight to the point, but always think before you speak. If possible, show proof or statistics that validate your proposal. Your ideas are more readily acceptable if they are supported by facts or explanations.

Don't close your mind to ideas that may sound unfeasible or ridiculous at first. Remember that many of the world's greatest discoveries have been previously rejected or even laughed at.

Choosing the right words is one of the most effective team communication skills. For example, you could say, "we have a challenge" instead of "we have a problem" to minimise stress or tension. You could say, "this is an awesome deal" instead of "this is a fair offer" to express your interest.

Be aware of the body language signals you're conveying while speaking. You may not have said anything offensive, but your body subconsciously communicates your inner emotions, so be aware of your actions and gestures all the time. When you speak, maintain eye contact and maintain a confident posture. Don't cross your arms, roll your eyes or purse lips as these imply disrespect.

Sometimes, having a sense of humour can be a great addition to your effective team communication skills. It overcomes boredom and dead air. But you should be keen enough to know when the right time is. You don't want to be humorous in the middle of a serious conversation.

Never criticise in public. If you have something to say that might offend or humiliate a member, restrain yourself. Talk to the person in private. It saves him face.

If you share these tips on utilising effective team communication skills to other members, don't be surprised on how quickly your team can accomplish its goals.

1. *Don't make assumptions:* All too often we assume the way we like to communicate is the way others like to as well. Not true! Instead of assuming you know, begin by observing how your team members communicate with other people. Do they tend to socialise before getting down to business, or are do they tend to be very direct. Observing will give you clues as to how your team prefers to communicate in a given situation. You can then adapt your management style to meet the needs of each individual member.
2. *Confirm your understanding:* It is vital to understand why people work the way they do. We know that observing is not enough, so the next logical step is to ask them. How often do we ask our team members how they prefer to work? Hardly ever, in my experience. The next step is to confirm your understanding by asking, "Am I correct, is this how you would like to work." I know what you must be thinking; this takes far too much time, probably time that you don't have. The time you invest now, in talking to your team is well worth the effort. The long-term result will be increased productivity, improved staff morale and you just might get your project in on time and within budget. It is equally important for you as the project manager to let your team know how you like to work. Speak up for your style.

3. *Give them what they need to succeed:* Give them what they need to succeed. People thrive in different types of environments. Some excel in a structured environment while others are motivated by recognition and reward. Some may even prefer a more challenging atmosphere. Understanding the environment they excel in will give you additional information on how to maximise your team.

Knowing what makes your people tick is what effective communication is all about. It will help you maximise productivity, efficiency and workplace harmony while minimising conflict, false assumptions and employee dissatisfaction.

Follow the tips given below and start practicing them within your team:

- Always respect all your fellow team members, irrespective of whether you are just a team member or a team leader.
- Ensure whether all the team members understand the project requirements thoroughly and know what the project targets are. Ask questions or have discussions to clarify the same.
- Organise regular team meetings to understand the doubts and queries of every team member and provide solutions accordingly.
- Keep every team member informed with the latest project updates or project issues.
- Define the role and responsibility of every team member clearly to avoid confusion or un-necessary re-work.
- When in a meeting or discussion, let every one have their turn to speak and suggest. It is of no use if you alone keep talking and ignore what others have to say.

- Listen to others' opinions and use their suggestions if found to be effective. Listening plays a significant role in effective communication. Repeat others' words to acknowledge their point of views.
- Ask for feedbacks and suggestions from your team members.
- Always speak in a clear and slow manner. Give sound and logical reasoning to your opinions.
- Always be polite in your way of speaking and behaviour. Using rude tone or body language may bring upon negative feelings among the team members.
- Clear out personal differences and misunderstandings by speaking it out with the concerned person. Keeping it inside and harbouring grudges against one another may affect the team spirit and have a direct impact on the quality of your work.
- Make appropriate use of emails, telephones, voice messages and instant messengers while communicating with the fellow team members. Follow the professional etiquettes while writing emails, greeting over telephones, leaving voice-mails and sending instant messages. These modes of communication also have a lot of importance in today's work place.
- Avoid using unpleasant words, expressions, giving out sensitive and confidential information while using the above modes of communication.
- Display acknowledgement and appreciation through face to face interaction or electronic modes when a team member performs well. Just a pat on the back, a warm handshake or two lines of an appreciation mail can have a great impact to motivate a team member.

- When appreciated or praised, thank the person in a polite and sophisticated manner. Avoid continuous rejoicing about your personal success. This might create an uncomfortable situation for your other team members.
- Always have a friendly attitude towards each other. Help others in need and you will get back others' help when you require the same.
- Deal with tense situations with a calm mind. If words of any team member make you angry try to keep a cool head and put your point forward. Avoid using harsh words in return.
- Avoid blaming others continuously when any work is not done. Instead, try to find out the root cause and see to it that it is not repeated in future.
- Find out if any team member is facing any problem and have a discussion with him/her to address the issue. Speaking and constant interaction with each other always help in developing a healthy team spirit.

DEVELOPING THE TEAM'S COMMUNICATIONS STRATEGY

The biggest issue for virtual teams is communications. A critical task for team leaders is to engage your team in creating an effective communications strategy. How can we create and follow a communications strategy for our team which adds value rather than creating overload? Too much communication about the wrong things is just as problematic as too little communication about important things.

- What, when are we going to communicate?
- Where and how will we communicate?
- Who will play what roles in the team's communications?

One way to start developing a communications strategy is to look at the nature of the different kinds of work the team will be doing and what kind of communication is needed to support that work.

There is a continuum which describes how individuals on the team are working from autonomously to interdependently. For example, there may be some tasks unique to a specific country which team members can do on their own without interacting with anyone else on the team. Other product-related projects may require more collaboration among team members in different parts of the region.

Another continuum can describe whether the patterns of our work—the problems, the tasks, the day-to-day activities—are repetitive and routine, whether these patterns are changing, or whether new patterns are emerging.

The nature of communications among the team about different parts of the work—including the frequency, the volume, and the degree of interactivity—is different depending on where that work falls in the matrix.

8

MAINTAINING QUALITY IN TEAM

Quality is primarily viewed in terms of corporate culture, multi-departmental ad-hoc task forces and the salvation of entire companies. Quality has become the philosophers' stone of management practice with consultants and gurus vying to charm lead-laden corporations into gold-winning champions. Stories abound of base companies with morose workers and mounting debts being transformed into happy teams and healthy profits; never a day goes by without a significant improvement, a pounds-saving suggestion or a quantum leap in efficiency. With this professed success of "Quality" programmes, there has evolved a proscriptive mythology of correct practise which has several draw backs:

- The edicts call for nothing less than a company wide, senior-management led programme.
- The adherence to a single formula has a limited effect, precludes innovation outside these boundaries, and reduces the differentiation which such programmes profess to engender.
- The emphasis on single-task, specially formed groups shifts the focus away from the ordinary, daily bread-and-butter.

Of course, these criticisms do not invalidate the ideas of Quality but are simply to suggest that the principles might well be viewed from a new angle—and applied at a different level.

THE CUSTOMER

In simple terms, attaining Quality has something to do with satisfying the expectations of the customer. Concern for the wishes and needs of customers becomes the focus for every decision. What the customer wants, the company provides. This is not philanthropy, this is basic survival. Through careful education by competitors, the customer has begun to exercise spending power in favour of quality goods and services; and while quality is not the sole criterion in selecting a particular supplier, it has become an important differentiator.

If one ball-point runs dry in one month and another ball-point lasts for three then the second ball-point is the make which the customer will buy again and which he/she recommends to others—even if it costs a little more. The makers of the first ball-point may have higher profit margins, but eventually no sales; without quality in the product, a company sacrifices customers, revenue and ultimately its own existence. In practical terms, Quality is that something extra which will be perceived by the customer as a valid reason for either paying more or for buying again.

In the case where the product is a service, Quality is equated with how well the job is done and especially with whether the customer is made to feel good about the whole operation. In this respect Quality often does cost more, but the loss is recouped in the price customers are prepared to pay and in the increase of business.

RELIABILITY

The clearest manifestation of Quality is in a product's reliability: that the product simply works. To prevent problems from arising after the product is shipped, the quality must be checked before-hand—and the best time to check quality is throughout the whole design and manufacturing cycle. The old method of quality control was to test the completed product and then to rework to remove the problems. Thus while the original production time was short, the rework time was long. The new approach to quality simply asserts that if testing becomes an integral part of each stage of production, the production time may increase but the rework time will disappear. Further, you will catch and solve many problems which the final "big-bang" quality-check would miss but which the customer will find on the first day.

To achieve this requires an environment where the identification of errors is considered to be "a good thing", where the only bad bugs are the ones which got away. One of the most hallowed doctrines of Quality is that of zero defects. "Zero defects" is a focus, it a glorious objective, it is the assertion that nothing less will suffice and that no matter how high the quality of a product, it can still be improved. It is a paradox in that it is an aim which is contrary to reason, and like the paradoxes of many other religions it holds an inner truth. This is why the advocates of Quality often seem a little crazy: they are zealots.

PEOPLE AS RESOURCE

While Quality has its own reward in terms of increased long-term sales, the methods used to achieve this Quality also have other benefits. In seeking to improve the quality of the product, manufacturers have found that the people best placed to make substantial contributions are the workforce: people are the most valuable resource. It is this shift in perspective from the management to the workforce which is the most significant consequence of the search for quality. From it has arisen a new managerial philosophy aimed at the empowerment of the workforce, decision-making by the front line, active worker involvement in the company's advancement; and from this new perspective, new organisational structures have evolved, exemplified in "Quality Circles".

Without digressing too much, it is important to examine the benefits of this approach. For such delegation to be safely and effectively undertaken, the management has to train the workforce; not necessarily directly, and not all at once, but often within the Quality Circles themselves using a single "facilitator" or simply peer-coaching. The workforce had to learn how to hold meetings, how to analyse problems, how to take decisions, how to present solutions, how to implement and evaluate change. These traditionally high-level managerial prerogatives are devolved to the whole staff. Not only does this develop talent, it also stimulates interest. Staff begin to look not only for problems but also for solutions. Simple ideas become simply implemented: the secretary finally gets the filing cabinet moved closer to the desk, the sales meetings follow an agenda, the software division creates a new bulletin board for the sports club. The environment is created where people see problems and fix 'em.

Larger problems have more complex solutions. One outcome of the search for Quality in Japan is the system of Just-In-Time flow control. In this system, goods arrive at each stage of the manufacturing process just before they are needed and are not made until they are needed by the next stage. This reduces storage requirements and inventory costs of surplus stock. Another outcome has been the increased flexibility of the production line. Time to change from one product run to the next was identified as a major obstacle in providing the customer with the desired range of products and quantities, and so the whole workforce became engaged in changing existent practices and even in redesigning the machinery.

THE LONG-TERM

The repeat-sale and recommendation are more important than this month's sales figures; staff training and development remain in place despite immediate schedule problems; the product's reliability is paramount even over time-to-market. Time is devoted today to saving time in the future and in making products which work first and every time.

TEAM QUALITY

While the salvation of an entire corporation may rest primarily with Senior Management, the fate of a team rests with the Team Leader. The Team Leader has the authority, the power to define the micro-culture of the work team. It is by the deliberate application of the principles of Quality that the Team Leader can gain for the team the same benefits which Quality can provide for a corporation.

The best ideas for any particular team are likely to come from them—the aim of the Team Leader must be to act as a catalyst through prompts and by example; the following are possible suggestions.

Getting Started

There will be no overnight success. To be lasting, Quality must become a habit and a habit is accustomed practise. This takes time and training—although not necessarily formal training but possibly the sort of reinforcement you might give to any aspect of good practise. To habituate your staff to Quality, you must first make it an issue. Here are two suggestions.

The first idea is to become enthusiastic about one aspect at a time, and initially look for a quick kill. Find a problem and start to talk about it with the whole team; do not delegate it to an individual but make it an issue for everybody. Choose some work-related problem like "how to get the right information in time" and solicit everybody's views and suggestions—and get the problem solved. Demand urgency against a clear target. There is no need to allocate large amounts of resource or time to this, simply raise the problem and make a fuss. When a solution comes, praise it by rewarding the whole team, and ensure that the aspects of increased efficiency/productivity/calm are highlighted since this will establish the criteria for "success". Next, find another problem and repeat.

The second idea is the regular weekly meeting to discuss Quality. Of course meetings can be complete time wasters, so this strategy requires care. The benefits are that regularity will lead to habit, the formality will provide a simple opportunity for the expression of ideas, and the inclusion of the whole group at the meeting will emphasize the collective responsibility. By using the regular meeting, you can establish the "ground rules" of accepted behaviour and at the same time train the team in effective techniques.

One problem is that the focus on any one particular issue may quickly loose its efficacy. A solution is to have frequent shifts in focus so that you maintain the freshness and enthusiasm. Further benefits are that continual shifts in emphasis will train your team to be flexible, and provide the opportunity for them to raise new issues. The sooner the team takes over the definition of the "next problem", the better.

Initial Phases

The initial phases are delicate. The team will be feeling greater responsibility without extra confidence. Thus you must concentrate on supporting their development. Essentially you will be their trainer in management skills. You could get outside help with this but by undertaking the job yourself, you retain control: you mould the team so that they will reflect your own approach and use your own criteria. Later they will develop themselves, but even then they will understand your thinking and so your decisions.

One trap to avoid is that the team may focus upon the wrong type of problem. You must make it clear any problem which they tackle should be:

- Related to their own work or environment.
- Something which they can change.

This precludes gripe sessions about wages and holidays.

As with all group work, the main problem is clarity. You should provide the team with a notice board and flip-charts specifically for Quality problems. These can then be left on display as a permanent record of what was agreed. If you can, steer the group first to some problem which has a simple solution and with obvious (measurable) benefits. A quick, sharp success will motivate.

TEAM BUILDING

To succeed, a Quality push must engage the enthusiasm of the entire team; as Team Leader, you must create the right atmosphere for this to happen. Many aspects of team building can be addressed while Quality remains the focus.

You must create the environment where each team member feels totally free to express an idea or concern and this can only be done if there is no stigma attached to being incorrect. No idea is wrong—merely non-optimal. In each suggestion there is at least a thread of gold and someone should point it out and, if possible, build upon it. Any behaviour which seeks laughter at the expense of others must be swiftly reprimanded.

One crude but effective method is to write down agreed ground rules and to display them as a constant reminder for everyone, something like:

- All criticism must be kind and constructive.
- All our-problems are all-our problems.
- Bugs Wanted: Dead or Alive (but not for long).
- If it saves time later, do it now.

Another method is to constantly talk about the group as the plural pronoun: "we decided", "we can do this", "we'll get back to you". This is especially effective if it is used in conversation with outsiders (especially management) within ear-shot of the team. Praise and reward the whole team; get the team wider fame by a success story in an internal newspaper.

Most importantly, you must enable failure. If the team is unable to try out ideas without rebuke for errors, then the scope of their solutions will be severely limited. Instead, a failure should be an opportunity to gain knowledge and to praise any safeguards which were included in the plan.

Mutual Coaching

An important aspect of team interaction is the idea of mutual support. If you can instill the idea that all problems are owned by the entire team then each member will be able to seek help and advice when needed from every other team member. One promoter of this is to encourage mutual coaching. If one team member knows techniques or information which would be useful to the rest, then encourage him/her to share it. Specifically this will raise the profile, confidence and self-esteem of the instructor at the same time as benefiting the entire group. And if there is one member who might never have anything useful to impart—send him/her to a conference or training session to find something.

Statistics

One of the central tenets of Quality programmes is the idea of monitoring the problem being addressed: Statistical Quality Control. Quite simply, if you can't measure an improvement, it probably isn't there. Gathering statistics has several benefits in applying Quality:

- It identifies (the extent of) the problem.
- It allows progress to be monitored.
- It provides an objective criterion for the abandonment of an idea.
- It can justify perceived expense in terms of observed savings/improvements.
- It motivates staff by providing a display of achievement and, of course, some problems simply disappear when you try to watch them.

The statistics must be gathered in an objective and empirical manner, the outcome should be a simple table or graph regularly updated to indicate progress, and these results must be displayed where all the team can watch. For example, if your team provides product support, then you might monitor and graph the number of repeat enquiries or the average response time. Or if you are in product development, you might want to monitor the number of bugs discovered.

In the long-term, it may be suitable to implement the automatic gathering of statistics on a wide range of issues such as complaints, bug reports, machine down-time, etc. Eventually these may either provide early warning of unexpected problems, or comparative data for new quality improvement projects. It is vital, however, that they focus upon an agreed problem and not upon an individual's performance or else all the positive motivation of staff involvement will be lost.

Projects

Clarity of purpose—this is the key to success. You need a simple, stated objective which everybody understands and which everybody can achieved.

Any plan to improve the quality or effectiveness of the group must contain:

— The objective.

— The method.

— The statistical display for monitoring the outcome.

— The agreed criteria for completion or curtailment.

By insisting on this format, you provide the plan-owners with a simple mechanism for peer recognition and yet enable them to manage their own failure with grace. For a small established team, the "customer" includes any other part of the company with which the team interacts. Thus any themes regarding customer satisfaction can be developed with respect to these so called internal customers. In the end, the effectiveness of your team will be judged by the reports of how well they provide products for others.

A simple innovation might be for a member of your team to actually talk to someone from each of these internal customer groups and to ask about problems. The interfaces are usually the best place to look for simply solved problems. The immediate benefit may be to the customer, but in the long run better communications will lead to fewer misunderstandings and so less rework.

BUILDING QUALITY

Quality costs less than its lack; look after the pennies and the profits will take care of themselves. To build a quality product, you must do two things:

- Worry the design and the procedures.
- Include features to aid quality checking.

It is a question of attitude. If one of the team spots a modification in the design or the procedures which will have a long term benefit, then that must be given priority over the immediate schedule. The design is never quite right; you should allocate time specifically to discussing improvement. In this you should not aim at actual enhancements in the sense of added features or faster performance, but towards simplicity or predicting problem areas. This is an adjunct to the normal design or production operations—the extra mile which lesser teams would not go.

Many products and services do not lend themselves to quality monitoring. These should be enhanced so that the quality becomes easily tracked. This may be a simple invitation for the "customer" to comment, or it could be a full design modification to provide self-checking or an easy testing routine. Any product whose quality can not be tracked should naturally become a source of deep anxiety to the whole team—until a mechanism is devised.

One of the least-used sources of quality in design and production in the engineering world is documentation. This is frequently seen as the final inconvenience at product release, sometimes even delegated to another (non-technical) group—yet the writing of such documentation can be used as an important vehicle for the clarification of ideas. It also protects the group from the loss of any single individual.

In devising a mechanism for monitoring quality, many teams will produce a set of test procedures. As bugs emerge, new procedures should be added which specifically identify this problem and so check the solution. Even when the problem is solved the new procedures should remain in the test set; the problem may return or the procedure may catch another. Essentially the test set should grow to cover all known possibilities of error and its application should, where possible, be automated.

Role Change

As your team develops, your role as leader changes subtly. You become a cross between a priest and a rugby captain, providing the vision and the values while shouting like crazy from the centre of the field. Although you retain the final say, the team begins to make decisions. The hardest part, as with all delegation, is in accepting the group decision even though you disagree. You must never countermand a marginal decision. If you have to over-rule the team, it is imperative that you explain your reasons very clearly so that they understand the criteria; this will both justify your intervention and couch the team in good decision-making practices.

Another role which you assume is that of both buffer and interface between the team and the rest of the company: a buffer in that you protect the team from the vagaries of less enlightened managers; an interface in that you keep the team informed about factors relevant to their decisions. Ultimately, the team will be delegating to you (!) tasks which only you, acting as manager, can perform on its behalf.

Quality for Profit

By applying the principles of Quality to an established team, the Team Leader can enjoy the benefits so actively sought by large corporations. The key is the attitude—and the insistence on the primacy of Quality. As a Team Leader, you have the power to define the ethos of your staff; by using Quality as the focus, you also can accrue its riches.

How to Select a Quality Team Building Provider

In the end we discuss these questions. These questions are based upon research from corporate clients and the qualities that they demand from a professional provider. First and foremost, it is important to remember that quality operators with genuine industry experience do exist. Unfortunately many band wagon riders (usually well meaning out-doorsy types or simply unskilled operators) have muddied the waters leaving a trail of disappointed clients in their wake.

A good operator will welcome these questions and should be able to answer them with confidence (it will even give some modest ones a chance to show off). The answers to these should assist in making your decision.

1. How many years have you been in operation as a dedicated corporate facilitator?

It is important to know that your provider has genuine experience in tailoring and delivering programmes for corporate clients. Trading off simple sports activities or games and then attempting complex corporate events can be a dangerous error for inexperienced providers. Make sure that their experience includes substantial contact and a proven track record with a range of corporate clients.

2. Do you tailor programmes to meet the clients needs?

An experienced operator should have a substantial repertoire of methodologies, programme options and concepts. The tailoring of an event should involve building the programme from scratch to suit the clients specific aims and objectives (not just pushing the standard off the shelf package). Ask questions about how the provider has actually tailored programme elements to dovetail with specific client aims such as change initiatives, process re-design, product developments etc.

3. Do you have professional facilitators?

Beware of those who simply round up a few mates, put them in bright shirts, and then expect them to deliver programmes to a corporate client. Unfortunately, great events don't come that easily. The word facilitator does get thrown around quite a lot. Enthusiastic hotel recreation staff, outdoor enthusiasts or a few mates do not necessarily make excellent corporate level facilitators. Ask how many facilitators actually work with the organisation full-time/part-time, what experience they have and if possible actually speak with some of them to gauge their ability. Make sure they know what they are doing. After all you don't want just anyone running around with your team. The skills, experience and training of the genuine article don't happen overnight or come that easily.

4. What internal systems and infrastructure do you have?

In theory, anyone claiming to offer corporate development services to the business world should be able to run a professional business operation him or herself. You should be satisfied that sufficient systems and support staff are in place to ensure that what has been promised to you will actually be delivered on time, in the right place and in the right way. Good QA doesn't go astray when providing any form of event.

5. Do you have comprehensive public liability insurance?

Professional operators wouldn't dream of taking a corporate group for a stroll to the corner store without this under their belt. In fact, a good operator should never need to call upon it, but it is a useful gauge of an operator's credibility whilst protecting both the client and themselves. If a major insurance company is satisfied with their level of expertise then at least you can make some judgments for yourself with this as a sound basis. Be especially aware of only partial or insufficient coverage in this area.

6. What theoretical knowledge do you have?

Just being able to coil a rope or burst with charisma doesn't necessarily equip someone with the skills to lock horns with a company's senior management or HRD team. An organisation providing corporate development should have within their own team some repository of management wisdom or at least the psychological basics. Even for a fun conference programme, it is nice to know that your provider has some idea about how the client and their people operate. Make sure that they are not all talk and no substance.

7. What is your C & I track record?

Conference and Incentive based events are often a world apart from standard outdoor-experiential training programmes. A good grounding in both structured team and management development programmes and C & I events, is useful. Ensure that your provider knows what is expected within a C & I environment.

8. Can we see some client testimonials?

Request actual testimonials of clients who have engaged this provider to deliver an event or a programme. If you are uncertain, ask to speak to a range of past clients with needs similar to yours. This should not pose a problem to an experienced operator.

9. Do you have a permanent stock of good equipment?

Whether the delegates are on a resort lawn for half an hour or in the wilderness for ten days, good gear is essential. Safety is an obvious issue that cannot be undervalued, but there are also some others. A good stock of clean, well-maintained and appropriate props and equipment helps to ensure smooth and professional delivery. It also demonstrates a level of commitment from the operator as a serious provider of team event services.

10. How are your concepts/activities developed?

A good operator will have developed their own range of concepts and activities that can be drawn upon to target a client's specific aims or to simulate a required situation or theme. Many borrow from a fairly standard range of concepts, which creates a risk of the client repeating tired old games and activities. Creativity and innovation is fairly important in a C & I environment so ensure that your provider has some original concepts and not just faded copies of someone else's.

9

TEAM EFFECTIVENESS

Team effectiveness refers to the system of getting people in a company or institution to work together effectively. The idea behind team effectiveness is that a group of people working together can achieve much more than if the individuals of the team were working on their own. Team effectiveness is determined by a number of factors, such as:

- *The right mix of skills:* Team effectiveness depends in part on bringing together people who have different skills that somehow complement each other. This can mean different technical abilities or communication skills. In fact, teaming up people who share the exact same characteristics is often a recipe for disaster. Team effectiveness depends on people taking on different roles in a group setting. If there is no agreement on who does what in the group, it is unlikely that the team will prosper.
- *The right motivation:* Team effectiveness is directly linked to the interest that the group has on the project. If the job is too easy or too difficult, or if the rewards for achieving the end result do not seem worth the effort, the team may end up working half-heartedly in the project. The task should also have a clear outcome. Working towards

a specific goal enhances team effectiveness significantly.

- *The ability to solve conflicts without compromising the quality of the project:* Team work has one major downfall. Sometimes groups end up making decisions they know are not in the best interest of the project, just so they can keep the process moving. Conflict is innate to any work done in groups, and should be taken as part of the challenge rather than as something to be avoided by compromising. Team effectiveness should be increased, not compromised, through conflict.

One way to enhance team effectiveness is to agree beforehand on a code of conduct. As conflicts arise, it is important to know how to deal with them. What is allowed and what is not? How will the team deal with disagreements? Is open discussion favoured or will the group vote on major decisions? Knowing what to expect and having the plan will make the process of working in group much easier.

When team members work well together, there us little they cannot accomplish. If your team is not winning championships, there's a way to find out:

- What's working right about your team,
- What's not working the way it should, and
- What to work on to "get back in the game?"

TEAM EFFECTIVENESS USING THE SCALED COMPARISON

Team Effectiveness is a proven and practical diagnostic tool for assessing team effectiveness and improving work group performance.

- Team Effectiveness gives the team a very precise and reliable consensus as to what team members see going well and what needs improvement.

- Team Effectiveness helps team members to very quickly pinpoint the gap between where they are and where they need to be.
- With Team Effectiveness, all team members participate in team improvement through a sharing of their views about team performance and needed improvement.
- Assessment with Team Effectiveness provides a level of clarity and precision that just isn't possible with interviews or other qualitative data collection tools.
- Unlike other diagnostic tools, Team Effectiveness works with teams as small as 5 to 7 members.

MEASURING TEAM EFFECTIVENESS

More than 30 years of studying teams in organisations has given us an understanding of how effective teams function, and how they differ from less effective teams. Team Effectiveness assesses all of the major components of effective work groups, employing multiple statements for each of a number of basic elements. Some of the elements are structural, and others are collaborative process elements:

(a) Structural elements
- Shared team vision
- Clear team goals
- Clear team roles
- Effective leadership behaviour

(b) Positive interdependent behaviours
- Effective decision making
- Encouragement of innovation
- Effective conflict management

- Natural collaboration
- Effective meeting management

Team building skills are critical for your effectiveness as a manager or entrepreneur. And even if you are not in a management or leadership role yet, better understanding of team work can make you a more effective employee and give you an extra edge in your corporate office.

A team building success is when your team can accomplish something much bigger and work more effectively than a group of the same individuals working on their own. You have a strong synergy of individual contributions. But there are two critical factors in building a high performance team.

The first factor in team effectiveness is the diversity of skills and personalities. When people use their strengths in full, but can compensate for each other's weaknesses. When different personality types balance and complement each other.

The other critical element of team work success is that all the team efforts are directed towards the same clear goals, the team goals. This relies heavily on good communication in the team and the harmony in member relationships.

In real life, team work success rarely happens by itself, without focused team building efforts and activities. There is simply too much space for problems. For example, different personalities, instead of complementing and balancing each other, may build up conflicts. Or even worse, some people with similar personalities may start fighting for authority and dominance in certain areas of expertise. Even if the team goals are clear and accepted by everyone, there may be no team commitment to the group goals or no consensus on the means of achieving those goals: individuals in the team just follow their personal opinions and move in conflicting directions. There may be a lack of trust and openness that blocks the critical communication and leads to loss of coordination in the individual efforts. And on and on. This is why every team needs a good leader who is able to deal with all such team work issues.

Here are some additional team building ideas, techniques, and tips you can try when managing teams in your situation.

- Make sure that the team goals are totally clear and completely understood and accepted by each team member.
- Make sure there is complete clarity in who is responsible for what and avoid overlapping authority. For example, if there is a risk that two team members will be competing for control in certain area, try to divide that area into two distinct parts and give each more complete control in one of those parts, according to those individual's strengths and personal inclinations.
- Build trust with your team members by spending one-on-one time in an atmosphere of honesty and openness. Be loyal to your employees, if you expect the same.
- Allow your office team members build trust and openness between each other in team building activities and events. Give them some opportunities of extra social time with each other in an atmosphere that encourages open communication. For example, in a group lunch on Friday. Though be careful with those corporate team building activities or events in which socialising competes too much with someone's family time.
- For issues that rely heavily on the team consensus and commitment, try to involve the whole team in

the decision making process. For example, via group goal setting or group sessions with collective discussions of possible decision options or solution ideas. What you want to achieve here is that each team member feels his or her ownership in the final decision, solution, or idea. And the more he or she feels this way, the more likely he or she is to agree with and commit to the decided line of action, the more you build team commitment to the goals and decisions.

— When managing teams, make sure there are no blocked lines of communications and you and your people are kept fully informed.

Even when your team is spread over different locations, you can still maintain effective team communication. Just do your meetings online and slash your travel costs.

— Be careful with interpersonal issues. Recognise them early and deal with them in full.

— Don't miss opportunities to empower your employees. Say thank you or show appreciation of an individual team player's work.

— Don't limit yourself to negative feedback. Be fare. Whenever there is an opportunity, give positive feedback as well.

Finally, though team work and team building can offer many challenges, the pay off from a high performance team is well worth it.

Measures of Team Effectiveness

Many organisations depend on teams to deliver—effective team working is therefore essential and assessment against seven dimensions can help to stay ahead of the game.

Teams need to be able to measure their own effectiveness in team working for two reasons:

1. Identify where things are wrong, quickly, in order to put them right.
2. Know when they are doing OK so they can get on with their work confidently.

Therefore, teams need a simple framework to guide them in checking that they are effective in the ways they need to be. One simple framework is called PERFORM—an acronym for the seven dimensions of effectiveness it comprises.

Productivity (or Outcomes)

Most important of the dimensions because it is about whether the team is getting the job done.

— Is it achieving its goals?

— Are its customers satisfied?

It can be useful to gather data to make an accurate assessment. However, teams are often very insightful and very honest with themselves about whether they are achieving what they need to do, as fast as they need to and to the standard they need to.

Empathy

This dimension considers whether team members feel comfortable with each other. It is important because if they do not, it can drain energy and creativity, which affects performance. Empathy is strongly related to the ability of the team to communicate effectively about difficult issues. It is not about being close friends or having lots of warm feelings in this context.

— Do the team members feel comfortable with each other?

Roles and Goals

This dimension relates to individuals knowing what their role is and how it fits in with others' roles on the team. Team tasks can fall through the cracks if people are not clear who should be taking responsibility for them, or if they don't know where their responsibility ends and another begins.

Flexibility

This dimension considers whether the team is responsive to outside influence and contribution. Some teams develop a rigid 'fortress-like' way of operating which can limit its functioning. Team members should ask themselves:

- How do they respond when the goalposts move?
- How much communicating do they do with teams around them?
- Do they listen and respond as well as tell?

Openness

This dimension relates to the free and ready communication between team members. It includes both information giving and opinion giving. Key questions are:

- Do people tell each other everything they need to know, including information about difficulties, mistakes, risks and problems?
- Do people say what they think?

Recognition

This dimension is important to the long-term health of the team and considers whether the team members celebrate their successes, both corporately and by praising each other. It may occur when people simply say

'Well Done' or 'That's a good idea' to each other or it may be a team treat. The important thing is whether team members feel their good work is recognised.

Morale

The word morale means many things to many people and is often a token word used by many organisations. Here it means that the team members want to be in the team, they are proud of it and of themselves in it—belonging to it makes them feel good. If morale is high, it is more likely that team members will achieve their potential and therefore, ultimately, so will the team.

Team effectiveness is essential for organisational success and through regular assessment and discussion, teams can diagnose issues and develop solutions to achieve their combined potential.

TEAM EFFECTIVENESS STRATEGIES

Leading a virtual team requires more than working on the team's project agenda. Teams which are unable to meet in person frequently because members are distributed geographically need additional help to support their team process so that they can act and feel like a team.

Here are several strategies team leaders can use which make a significant difference in team effectiveness.

- Make whole visible to everyone
- Provide "line of sight".
- Catalyse rich conversations.
- Amplify energy.
- Create tracks and footprints in physical space.

Get the whole team involved in the process of being conscious of making these things happen. That not only distributes the work but makes it more likely that opportunities to support these strategies won't be missed.

One way of involving the team is to share the list and talk about which one or two strategies would be worthwhile to work on for the next period of time. Develop a shared understanding and an image of what it would feel like if the team was successful in implementing the strategy. Brainstorm a list of ways to achieve goals related to the selected strategy. Be as concrete and specific as possible in identifying actions for team members and team leaders.

10

TEAM RISK MANAGEMENT

Team risk management defines the organisational structure and operational activities for collectively managing risks throughout all phases of the life cycle of a software-dependent development programme such that all individuals within the organisations, groups, departments, and agencies directly involved in the programme are participating team members. Team risk management practices bring together individuals within an organisation and between organisations to form working teams.

The team risk management approach is built upon the nine principles summarised in Table 10.1. These principles combine the risk management paradigm and the concepts of cooperative teams to form the foundation for a comprehensive set of processes, methods, and tools for managing risks.

Team risk management involves concurrent activities of partner organisations working together to manage programme risks. In the case of a software-dependent development programme awarded by the government to a primary contractor, there are two partner organisations: the government programme office and the contractor. Within team risk management, partner organisations participate in cooperative, inter-organisational "team" activities which are represented by the surface of the team risk management process sphere. Communication, which is represented by the core of the sphere, also interconnects the partners and represents intra-organisational as well as inter-organisational communication processes that are vital to effective team risk management.

Table 10.1: The Nine Principles of Team Risk Management

Principle	Effective risk management requires
1. Shared product vision	A shared vision for success based upon commonality of purpose, shared ownership, and collective commitment.
2. Forward-looking search for uncertainties	Thinking toward tomorrow, anticipating potential outcomes, identifying uncertainties, and managing programme resources and activities while recognising these uncertainties.
3. Open communications	A free flow of information at and between all programme levels through formal, informal, and impromptu communication and consensus-based processes.
4. Value of Individual perception	The individual voice which can bring unique knowledge and insight to the identification and management of risk.
5. Systems perspective	That software development be viewed within the larger systems-level definition, design, and development.
6. Integration into programme management	That risk management be an integral and vital part of programme management.
7. Proactive strategies	Proactive strategies that involve planning and executing programme activities based upon anticipating future events.

Contd...

Principle	*Effective risk management requires*
8. Systematic and adaptable methodology	A systematic approach that is adaptable to the programme's infrastructure and culture.
9. Routine and continuous processes	A continuous vigilance characterised by routine risk identification and management activities throughout all phases of the life cycle of the programme.

While team risk management has been presented in the context of a government/contractor relationship, the concept of team risk management is general. In this broader context, the approach encompasses any customer/supplier relationship such that the team risk management process sphere is divided into the upper hemisphere and the lower hemisphere. Each hemisphere may include multiple customer or supplier partner organisations.

Fundamentally, the implementation of team risk management in a government programme brings together the government and the contractor in a continuous and collective effort for success, where both are focused on managing programme risks.

TEAM RISK MANAGEMENT PROCESSES

The team risk management processes include continuous processes and a one-time process activity, the baseline risk assessment. The continuous processes of team risk management incorporate all five steps of the the risk management paradigm described above into four processes by combining the identification and analysis steps into the routine risk identification and analysis process. Similarly, the baseline risk assessment combines the identification and analysis steps of the paradigm into a single process activity that establishes the initial set of risks and initiates the continuous process activities.

The team review process defines cooperative risk management activities between the partner organisations. The baseline risk assessment is an intra-organisational process executed independently by each partner organisation involved in team risk management. The team review process is an inter-organisational process conducted jointly between the government and the contractor. The other continuous risk management processes are dualrole processes.

The nine principles of team risk management and the cooperative team approach provide the foundation for all of the team risk management activities, whether intra-organisational, interorganisational, or dual-role activities. Thus, while the inter-organisational processes are inherently team activities, the intra-organisational and dual-role processes also have a strong team character. This sense of "team" pervades all facets of the implementation of team risk management.

When team risk management is applied to a software-dependent development programme that has been awarded by the government to a prime development contractor, both the government office and the contractor concurrently execute the team risk management processes. Specifically, each conducts a baseline assessment and subsequently executes the continuous team risk management processes. The basic classifications of team risk management processes are summarised in Table 10.2.

The team reviews held throughout the life of the programme provide formal inter-organisational communication and coordination on programme risks. These joint government and contractor reviews include reviews of the status of risks, discussions of the risks, risk management activities and plans, and reviews of strategies for dealing with risks. Through these team reviews the government and contractor share perspectives, ideas, and objectives and arrive at a better understanding of the programme risks and objectives. These reviews are generally scheduled as part of routine programme reviews but can be convened as needed to address specific issues or as part of a key programme milestone.

Table 10.2. Process Classifications of Team Risk Management

	Classification	*Description*
1.	Continuous processes	The dual-role continuous risk management processes consist of the risk management process steps: identification, analysis, planning, tracking, and control as well as inter-organisational activities, including regularly scheduled team reviews as well as unscheduled informal meetings and communications.
2.	Baseline activities	The initial, one-time identification and analysis of activities that establish the baseline set of risks conducted by each partner organisation, government and contractor.

The baseline assessments establish the initial risk sets: one for the government programme office and one for the contractor. The risks identified in the baseline form the basis for the initial team event, the team review. This review combines the most important risks from both the government and the contractor into a programme-wide list, the Joint List of Risks. The Joint List of Risks is the focus of the joint "team" management efforts and represents the most important risks faced by the programme.

Following the baseline assessment, action planning is initiated. The action planning process defines and initiates specific actions for dealing with the risks. The tracking and control process steps monitor the results of the action plans and control the progress of the programme's risk management activities. The routine risk identification and analysis process step is a continuous activity, throughout both the government and contractor organisations, that identifies new or changing risks in the programme. All risks are incorporated into the action planning process, and are incorporated into the team review process as required. Team risk management is implemented as a routine, continuous, and integral part of programme management activities. Within this programme context, it provides the basis for joint (government/contractor) management of programme risks as well as the basis for individual organisations to manage risk.

Continuous Team Risk Management Process

Risks exist and emerge throughout the entire life-cycle of a programme; thus, the processes of identifying and managing risks must continue from the programme's inception. The continuous processes of team risk management, comprise a cyclic set of routine activities for managing risk. Collectively, these processes involve: identifying risks, periodically reviewing and analysing new risks, planning for the judicious application of resources to mitigate risks, tracking the status of risks and risk mitigation actions, controlling risks that turn into problems, and communicating about risks among all partners in the programme. The systematic methods that make up continuous team risk management processes can be adapted to any programme's infrastructure and culture through the modification of forms or instruments, the appropriate scheduling of activities, the integration of the methods into existing programme activities, or the adoption of the complete, unmodified set of processes, methods, and tools.

The primary cycle of activities in continuous team risk management has five parts as listed below and as briefly described in Table 10.3:

- Routine risk identification and analysis.
- Team reviews.
- Action planning.
- Tracking.
- Control.

All of the activities are tied together through informal and formal communication processes. These activities enhance the cooperative interactions and trust between partners and team members, and build and reinforce the shared programme vision required for effective team risk management.

Table 10.3: Continuous Team Risk Management Methods, Tools, and Communication Characteristics

Team Risk Management Process	*Methods/Tools*	*Communication Characteristics*
(1)	(2)	(3)
Routine Risk Identification & Analysis	• routine risk form processing • periodic risk reporting • periodic individual interview session • periodic risk assessments	• non-judgmental • non-attribution • confidential • individual voice
Team Reviews	• comparison risk ranking • nominal group technique	• mutual understanding • consensus
Action Planning	• periodic technical reviews • review and assign • strategise	• mutual understanding • consensus on responsibilities
Tracking	• metrics • status indicators • triggers	• mutual understanding
Control	• risk corrections • risk action	• mutual understanding • consensus on actions

Except for team reviews, all of the continuous team risk management activities are included in a "core cycle" of processes. Team reviews provide the means for the government and the contractor to jointly decide on risk plans, responsibilities, and actions for managing risks, and for formally communicating information on the current progress of risk management activities in their respective organisations. Team reviews, then, are a method that can be viewed as being on the surface of the team risk management sphere, whereas the core cycle of activities–routine risk identification and analysis, action planning, tracking, and control–embody the risk paradigm processes and constitute the center of the team risk management sphere.

The core cycle begins with routine risk identification and analysis to identify new risks, proceeds to action planning for those risks, and is followed by the tracking and control of those risks. These activities are sequential for a given risk, but are continually overlapping programme activities in that there will always be risks in any one of these phases. Routine risk identification and analysis provides the means to identify new risks during the programme's life cycle and to perform a preliminary analysis on these risks. This can be on a voluntary basis where new risks are identified at any time by any person, but also includes periodic, more formal, reviews of the programme by a select set of knowledgeable personnel. Regardless of the specific method used, this process is a combined identification and preliminary analysis which results in a risk statement

Preliminary analysis includes:

- Estimation of significance (of the impact).
- Estimation of the likelihood of occurrence.
- Estimation of the time frame of occurrence (or need to take action).

— An indication of criticality (i.e., requires immediate management attention).

— A recommendation for resolution.

Periodic Risk Reporting

A second method for routine risk identification and analysis involves the periodic reporting of risk identification information. These risk identification status reports are generally included as part of the programme's normally scheduled reporting activities and may involve every individual or only selected key individuals working on the programme. This method asks that weekly, biweekly, or monthly, each individual involved in the programme submit a risk identification status report as part of routine status reporting. The risk identification status report may be the risk form or a summary risk identification section included within the programme's normal status report forms. The risk summary section should consist of a risk statement and its significance, likelihood, time frame, and criticality. If an individual has not identified a new risk then that information should be reported as well.

Baseline Risk Assessment

All of the baseline risk assessment activities are conducted by a trained risk assessment team. This assessment team may be part of the programme's parent organisation or may be independent of the organisation. If the assessment team comes from the parent organisation, it should be external to the programme being assessed. Regardless of the team's composition, training is important to effectively carry out the risk assessment process.

The initial process step in a baseline risk assessment, initiate, involves establishing a commitment on the part of the organisation's personnel to the team risk management process. The commitment involves the participation of personnel throughout the programme and provides an overview of the process to all of the participants involved and prepares them for their roles in that process. This presentation is the start of the "buy-in" that is so important to introducing change into an organisation.

BIBLIOGRAPHY

Alanna Jones, *Team-Building Activities for Every Group*, Rec Room Publishing, 2000.

Bradley J Sugars, *Instant Team Building (Instant Success)*, McGraw-Hill, 2005.

Brian Cole Miller, *Quick Team-Building Activities for Busy Managers: 50 Exercises That Get Results in Just 15 Minutes*, AMACOM, 2003.

Carl Larson and Frank LaFasto, *Teamwork: What Must Go Right/ What Can Go Wrong*, Sage Publications, 1998.

Chuck Kormanski and Andrew Mozenter, "A New Model of Team Building: A Technology for Today and Tomorrow," *Annual Handbook for Group Facilitators*, University Associates, 1987.

Deborah Mackin, *The Team-Building Tool Kit: Tips and Tactics for Effective Workplace Teams*, AMACOM, 2nd edition, 2007.

Gardner John W., *On Leadership*, NY: The Free Press; January 1990

Hackman, J. Richard Editor, *Groups That Work (and Those That Don't)*, Jossey-Bass, 1998.

Jon Katzenbach and Douglas Smith, *The Wisdom of Teams*, Harvard Business School Press, 1998.

Jack D. Orsburn, et.al., *Self-Directed Work Teams*, Business One Irwin, 1998.

John W. Newstrom, *The Big Book of Team Building: Quick, Fun Activities for Building Morale, Communication and Team Spirit*, McGraw-Hill Professional, 2008.

Ken Blanchard, *Group Development and Situational Leadership*, 1989.

Kinlaw, Dennis, *Handbook of Leadership Training Activities*, McGraw-Hill, New York, 1998.

Linda Moran, Ed Musselwhite and John Zenger, *Keeping Teams on Track*, Irwin, 1998.

Rodney Napier and Matti Gershenfeld, *Groups: Theory and Practice*, Houghton Mifflin, 1998.

Snow, Harrison, *Indoor/Outdoor Team Building Games for Trainers*, McGraw-Hill, New York, 1997.

Steven Phillips and Robin Elledge, *The Team Building Source Book*, Jossey-Bass/Pfeiffer, 1998.

Susan Albers Mohrman, Susan Cohen and Allan M. Mohrman, Jr., *Designing Team-Based Organizations*, Jossey-Bass, 1998.

Victor Vroom and Edward Deci, *Management and Motivation*, Penguin, 1970

William G. Dyer, et.al., *Team Building: Proven Strategies for Improving Team Performance*, Jossey-Bass; 4 edition, 2007.